P9-DHJ-095

UNIVERSITY ASSOCIATES
Publishers and Consultants

SERIES IN HUMAN RELATIONS TRAINING

A Handbook of Structured Experiences for Human Relations Training

Volume III
(Revised)

Edited by

J. WILLIAM PFEIFFER, Ph.D.
Human Relations Consultant
La Jolla, California

JOHN E. JONES, Ph.D.
Human Relations Consultant
La Jolla, California

UNIVERSITY ASSOCIATES
8517 Production Avenue
P.O. Box 26240
San Diego, California 92126

The materials that appear in this book may be freely reproduced for educational/training activities. There is no requirement to obtain special permission for such uses. We do, however, ask that the following statement appear on all reproductions:

Reproduced from
*A Handbook of Structured Experiences for
Human Relations Training, Volume III, Revised*
J. William Pfeiffer and John E. Jones, Editors
San Diego, CA: UNIVERSITY ASSOCIATES, Inc., 1974

This permission statement is limited to reproduction of materials for educational/training events. *Systematic or large-scale reproduction or distribution—or inclusion of items in publications for sale—may be done only with prior written permission.*

PREFACE TO THE REVISED EDITION

In the five years since the first volume of *A Handbook of Structured Experiences for Human Relations Training* appeared, we have accumulated considerable experience with these materials. In addition to the four volumes of the *Handbook*, we have developed a companion publication—*The Annual Handbook for Group Facilitators*. This editorial activity has been accompanied by a wide array of experiences in consulting and in laboratories and workshops where we have experimented with many variations. We have also received numerous contributions from group facilitators. Some of these have been incorporated into revisions of the *Handbook*.

The *Handbook* has been revised in content and re-designed to have a more durable cover. Type faces have been selected which will allow clear photo-reproduction, both at the same size and in enlargements.

The structured experiences that appear in this book are the "folk music" of human relations. They fall into three major categories: (1) unadapted "classic" experiences, (2) highly adapted experiences, and (3) innovated experiences. Like folk music, the origins of most of these structured experiences are difficult to trace. They have been passed from facilitator to facilitator by word-of-mouth, on scraps of paper, and on unsigned, undated mimeographed sheets.

We have made considerable effort to determine the authorship of these materials, but we continue to have concern about the accuracy of our research into finding the people who developed particular exercises. An interesting phenomenon occurs in the human relations training field that aggravates the authorship problem. A facilitator uses a structured experience or an instrument for several years, it becomes a part of his training repertoire, and he forgets where he originally obtained it. When he sees another facilitator using a version of it, he feels that he is not being acknowledged for something which he "owns." As one consultant put it, "I have been using my own version for such a long time, that I simply assumed it was the only one in the world."

Although the *Handbook* is copyrighted, there are few restrictions concerning the reproduction of its contents. Users should feel free to duplicate and/or modify the forms, charts, structured exercises, descriptions, and instruments for use in education/training designs. However, *reproduction of items from the book in publications for sale or large-scale distribution should be done only with the prior permission of the editors.* The intent is to make these materials widely available and useful. Occasionally someone asks whether we are concerned about this policy. Our response is that we wish more publishers would follow suit..It is widely known that copyrighted materials are duplicated for use in learning designs. We believe it is unnecessary to cause those who duplicate such materials to feel guilty.

This handbook is written by practitioners for practitioners. In the *Handbooks* and the *Annuals* we record the development of structured experiences, instruments, theoretical positions, and ideas for applications as they emerge. To that end we invite inquiries from facilitators about our policies regarding incorporating their work in future

v

publications. Users are encouraged to submit structured experiences, instruments they have developed, and papers they have written which might be of interest to practitioners in human relations training. In this manner, our Series in Human Relations Training serves a clearinghouse function for ideas developed by group facilitators.

J. William Pfeiffer
John E. Jones

La Jolla, California
October, 1973

ABOUT UNIVERSITY ASSOCIATES
PUBLISHERS AND CONSULTANTS

UNIVERSITY ASSOCIATES is an educational organization engaged in human relations training, research, consulting, publication, and both pre-service and in-service education. The organization consists of educational consultants and experienced facilitators in human relations, leadership training, and organization development.

In addition to offering general laboratory experiences, University Associates designs and carries out programs on a contractual basis for various organizations. These programs fall under the following areas of specialization: Human Relations Training, Leadership Development, Organization Development, Community Development, and Educational Research.

Structured experiences in University Associates publications are numbered consecutively. Structured experiences 1 through 24 are in *Volume I*, numbers 25 through 48 are in *Volume II*, numbers 49 through 74 in *Volume III*, 75 through 87 in *The 1972 Annual Handbook for Group Facilitators*, 88 through 100 in the *1973 Annual*, and 101 through 124 in *Volume IV*. These numbers are used for the same exercise when books are revised, even though the title of the exercise or some details may be changed.

TABLE OF CONTENTS

INTRODUCTION TO THE REVISED EDITION

Since its inception, University Associates has become involved with or had experience in nearly every facet of human relations training. With these experiences, we have grown personally and have found our philosophies to be evolving continuously as our awareness of the impact and methodology of human relations grows.

Spontaneous experiences within a group training setting may be valuable in terms of awareness expansion and emotional freedom. However, they may not produce as much personal growth and solid, transferable learning as does a structured experience, designed to focus on individual behavior, constructive feedback, processing, and psychological integration.

Our interest in providing a distinctive model of human relations training has resulted in an increasing orientation within our consulting activities, laboratories, and workshops toward experiences which will produce generally predictable outcomes. In designing experiences, we strive to examine specific needs of a client system or group and then develop learning situations to meet these needs. We believe that this concern for learning needs should be the minimum expectation of any individual participating in a training event. Therefore, all of our training designs incorporate structure to facilitate learning.

Our use of and experimentation with structured experiences have led to an interest in developing useful, uncomplicated questionnaires and other instruments. Each volume of the *Handbook* contains structured experiences that include instruments. Many commercially available instruments are being used more and more in our laboratory designs. We published *Instrumentation in Human Relations Training* by Pfeiffer and Heslin in June, 1973, to share information about the use of these materials. We find that the complementary use of structured experiences and instruments can create powerful learning environments. We encourage those in human relations training to become acquainted with this two-fold approach.

The adaptability of both structured experiences and instruments in creating highly functional training designs has emerged as a chief consideration in publishing materials. One norm in human relations training activities is innovation. Therefore, the structured experiences in these handbooks can easily be adapted to fit a particular training design. As one friend remarked of the handbook, "I use it all of the time, but I almost never do things the way you guys describe them."

Our awareness of the infinite variety of experiences which can be produced in adapting these materials becomes more specifically focused the longer we work in human relations. Therefore, in revising the *Handbook*, we have added a section entitled "Variations" to the structured experiences format. Hopefully, the variations we suggest will trigger other adaptation ideas.

In addition, we cross-reference experiences which supplement or complement each other. We also incorporate references to appropriate lecturettes and other materials from our *Annual Handbook for Group Facilitators*. The facilitator may use the "Notes" section in this book as a starting point for adaptation.

The purpose, then, of the *Handbook* is to share training materials we have found to be viable in training designs. Part of the experiences were originated within University Associates, and part were submitted by facilitators in the field. It is gratifying that facilitators around the world are using the *Handbook* and concur with the philosophy that sharing these valuable materials is more in the spirit of human relations theory than the stagnating concept of "ownership" of ideas.

As in other volumes of the *Handbook*, content is arranged, for the most part, in order of the increasing understanding, skill, and experience needed by the facilitator. The first structured experience, therefore, requires much less background of the facilitator than does the last. The earlier experiences generate less affect and less data than do those near the end of the book; consequently the facilitator needs less skill in processing to use them effectively and responsibly.

A concern we bring to all our training publications is the need for adequate processing of any human relations training experience, so that participants are able to integrate learning without stress generated by unresolved feelings and/or lack of understanding. At this point the expertise of the facilitator becomes crucial if the experience is to be responsive to the learning and emotional needs of the participants. The facilitator must decide whether he will be able to process successfully the data which emerges.

Any facilitator, regardless of his background, who is committed to the growth of individuals in his group can usefully employ these structured experiences. The choice of activities should be made by two criteria—the facilitator's competence and the participants' needs.

49. "WHO AM I?" VARIATIONS: A GETTING-ACQUAINTED ACTIVITY

Goal

To allow participants to become acquainted quickly in a relatively non-threatening way. (These variations may be especially appropriate for participants who have difficulty writing about themselves, as in "Who Am I?," *Vol. I*: Structured Experience 5.)

Group Size

Unlimited.

Time Required

Approximately forty-five minutes.

Materials

I. Sheets of paper, 12" × 20", one to be fastened around each participant's neck "bib-style," with a string.

II. Ball of string and scissors.

III. Pencils or felt-tipped markers.

Physical Setting

Large room in which participants may move freely.

Process

I. Participants receive the materials and are allowed ten minutes for any of the following activities to introduce themselves to fellow participants. The facilitator may choose one variation for all participants or allow participants to choose any variation they wish.

    1. Participants may draw a picture or pictures of themselves: a caricature, a cartoon strip, etc.

    2. Participants may draw a pie with different-sized wedges to illustrate

percentages of themselves devoted to certain life focuses—for example, a love-distribution pie or an energy pie.

   3. Participants may draw a "life line"—a graph of their lives to the present, showing high points—or a projected total life line which indicates where they are now.

   4. Participants may write a series of words, such as adjectives. Words might be selected through free association.

   5. Specialty groups, such as musicians, math engineers, or chemists, may identify themselves with their own symbols.

   6. Participants may draw pictures of animals, objects, or music with which they identify.

   7. Participants may write words to indicate their own values.

  II. Each participant ties his completed sheet around his neck.

 III. Participants circulate in cocktail-party fashion, but *without* speaking. (Background music is optional.)

 IV. The facilitator asks participants to move on to a new person every minute for a total of ten to fifteen "meetings."

  V. After this nonverbal phase, the participants are told to return to two or three people they thought would be interesting, based on their previous encounters. They may now speak to one another. They may be encouraged to ask questions they ordinarily would not ask.

Variations

  I. Instead of the question "Who am I?," participants can complete the open-ended statement "I am becoming the kind of person who . . ." or the sentence "I am pretending that . . . ." (It is important that at least ten different responses be called for, so that participants move beyond superficial self-disclosure.)

 II. Participants may be asked to avoid giving demographic data in their answers. The facilitator may illustrate by pointing out the difference between "What am I?" (husband, father, counselor, etc.) and "Who am I?" (tense, a taker of risks, managing myself toward openness, etc.).

 III. Self-descriptive adjectives can be called for instead of answers to the question. A second column of adjectives could be in response to the question "How would I like to be?"

 IV. Participants may be permitted to speak in Process step III.

  V. After the processing, participants can post their sheets on a wall, so that all the getting-acquainted data are available for study at all times. Persons may edit their sheets at any time during the training event.

VI. As a closure activity, participants may be instructed to write what they learned during the training. The content may be varied. For example, in a personal growth laboratory the topic could be "What I learned about me"; in a leadership/management development laboratory, the topic could simply be "What I learned" or "What I am going to do differently."

Similar Structured Experiences: *Vol. I:* Structured Experience **5, 13, 20;** *Vol. II:* **42, 47;** *'73 Annual:* **87, 88, 90, 99;** *Vol. IV:* **101.**
Lecturette Sources: *'73 Annual:* "Johari Window," "Risk-Taking."

Notes on the use of "Who Am I?" Variations:

50. BEHAVIOR DESCRIPTION TRIADS: READING BODY LANGUAGE

Goals

I. To practice describing nonverbal behavior objectively, without interpretation.

II. To study the body-language messages that accompany verbalization.

III. To alert group members to the variety of signals they use to communicate.

Group Size

Unlimited number of triads.

Time Required

Approximately fifteen minutes.

Physical Setting

A room large enough to permit triads to work separately, without distraction.

Process

I. The facilitator briefly discusses the goals of the activity.

II. Triads are formed.

III. Participants in each triad identify themselves as A, B, or C.

IV. *Round 1.* Participants A and B stand facing each other. For two minutes A describes all of the nonverbal behavior of B. (The facilitator may demonstrate by rapidly describing the body language of another person.) Participant C acts as a referee to insure that A is nonevaluative and noninterpretive in his description. The triad then discusses Round 1. Feelings, interpretations, and other observations may emerge.

V. *Round 2.* The process is repeated, with B describing C's behavior and A acting as referee. Then they discuss the experience.

VI. *Round 3.* The process is repeated again, with C describing A and with B acting as referee. Then they discuss the experience.

VII. Triads link up with one or two other triads to process the exercise. During this phase of the meeting, participants should observe all messages emitted, both verbal and nonverbal.

Variations

I. Participants can be instructed to add their interpretations to their observations.

II. Participants can focus on symbols, instead of nonverbal behavior. They may describe (and interpret) clothes, hair, jewelry, etc.

III. A two-person interchange can be videotaped for replay before an audience, which can read the body language of the participants. The sound can be turned off during the replay.

Similar Structured Experiences: *Vol. I:* Structured Experience **1, 8;** *Vol. II:* **42;** *'72 Annual:* **75;** *'73 Annual:* **87.**
Lecturette Sources: *'72 Annual:* "Communication Modes: An Experiential Lecture"; *'73 Annual:* "Conditions which Hinder Effective Communication."

Notes on the use of "Behavior Description Triads":

Structured Experience 50

51. EMPTY CHAIR: AN EXTENDED GROUP DESIGN

Goal

To allow all participants to become involved voluntarily in a group-on-group experience when the size of the total group makes discussion impractical.

Group Size

Unlimited. (The example described here is based on a total group of more than fifteen participants.)

Time Required

Open.

Physical Setting

Circle of seven chairs in the center of the room, with an outer circle of chairs for the rest of the group.

Process

I. The facilitator solicits six volunteers for an inner-circle group to sit in the chairs provided. (This leaves one vacant chair.)

II. Individuals from the outer group are told they may join the inner group, one at a time, when they want to contribute some data or to clarify inner-group data. (Remaining outer-group members *may not* talk.) An outer-group individual may stay in the inner group only for the time required to process his input and then he must vacate the seventh chair to make room for another outer-group individual. Under no circumstances may anyone become a permanent member of the inner group. The facilitator may need to enforce this rule. It is not necessary for an outer-group member to be in the inner circle at all times; outer-group members may participate when they wish.

Variations

I. The permanent members of the inner circle may be polarized: In a university setting, for instance, they may consist solely of deans and radical students, while members of the outer circle may be professors and conservative students.

II. The permanent members of the inner circle may be hierarchical: In a business setting, for instance, they may consist solely of managers, while the outer circle contains only hourly employees.

III. The number of empty chairs in the inner circle may be varied. The inner circle may contain enough chairs for the total group.

IV. The facilitator may require that the person who occupies the empty chair wait for a "natural" opening in the discussion to offer his comments. Members of the inner circle may be instructed to "open the gate" for that person.

V. After about thirty minutes the inner and outer groups can be reversed, or a new inner group can be selected.

VI. Members of the inner group may be free to leave the circle, allowing more than one outer-group member at one time to join the inner circle.

Similar Structured Experiences: *Vol. I:* Structured Experience **6**; *'72 Annual:* **76, 79**; *'73 Annual:* **92**.
Lecturette Source: *'73 Annual:* "Design Considerations in Laboratory Education."

Notes on the use of "Empty Chair":

52. NOT-LISTENING: A DYADIC ROLE-PLAY

Goals

I. To allow participants to experience the frustration of not being heard.

II. To promote listening readiness.

Group Size

Unlimited numbers of dyads.

Time Required

Approximately thirty minutes.

Materials

I. For each dyad, copies of the two roles to be played.

II. Newsprint and felt-tipped marker.

Physical Setting

A room large enough for the dyad members to confront each other in their respective roles, with minimum disturbance of other dyads.

Process

Note: This structured experience is intended to be the first activity in a training event. It should be followed by a success experience in effective listening (*e.g., Vol. I*: Structured Experience 8).

I. The facilitator discusses the goals of the activity.

II. The group forms dyads, and the facilitator gives each dyad a copy of each role. These may be devised by the facilitator; or, Not-Listening Role-Briefing Sheets (Option No. 1 or Option No. 2) may be used.

III. The dyads then have about three minutes to study their roles.

IV. All dyads should begin the exercise at the same time.

V. The facilitator makes sure that dyad participants are *not* listening to each other. He confronts those participants who appear to be doing so.

VI. When the facilitator feels that the group is experiencing maximal frustration (usually indicated by a sharp, sustained increase in noise), he stops the activity.

VII. The remaining time is spent listing participants' responses to the frustration. The group discusses these observations.

Variations

I. Participants can develop their own role-play situations.

II. Triads can be used, with the third person acting as an observer/judge, who notes evidence of frustration and enforces the "no-listening" rule.

III. As a part of step III, the total group can be divided in half, with all participants in each half preparing to play the same role. Subgroups can be formed to rehearse the role-play.

Similar Structured Experience: *Vol. I:* Structured Experience **8.**
Lecturette Source: *'73 Annual:* "Conditions Which Hinder Effective Communication."

Notes on the use of "Not-Listening":

Submitted by Harvey B. Karp, Old Dominion University, Norfolk, Virginia.

Structured Experience 52

NOT-LISTENING ROLE-BRIEFING SHEET (Option No. 1)

Chief Purchasing Agent

You have just been hired as the chief purchasing agent of a large corporation. Your title is Vice-President in Charge of Purchasing. You have a Ph.D. in economics from Harvard, have headed a presidential advisory board, and have published two books in your field. You see that the best way to bring order out of chaos is to centralize the purchasing operations, and quickly! You have decided that any purchase over $10,000 must be approved by the head office. You realize that the independent purchasing power of each plant has been jealously guarded. You are also aware that the peak buying season starts in three weeks.

You have decided that the only way to put this policy in operation in time is to visit each plant general manager, inform him of your plan, explain why it is necessary, and insist that it must be followed. You know you are going to meet some stiff opposition; however, *you* are the expert, and *you* have the power. You are determined you will not be sidetracked by minor objections; you are the only one who knows the total picture.

General Manager

You are the general manager of the second largest plant in a large corporation. You have been employed at this plant for twenty-seven years, starting as an office boy and working your way up through sales, purchasing, and production. You took over the top position three years ago. No one knows more about the inner workings of this plant than you. Last year, the home office gave a testimonial dinner for you to show its appreciation of the fine job you have done and are doing.

You just received a memo from the home office that a new chief purchasing agent has been hired, and the word is that he may try to centralize the purchasing operation. While this plan might look good on paper, you know that the strength of the corporation has always been its flexibility. The key to this flexibility has been management development and autonomous plant decisions.

You are aware that, if this new policy takes effect, it will not only reduce the plant's flexibility, but it will signal an end to the power now held by general managers.

You are determined that the chief purchasing agent will not enforce his policy. He probably means well, but he just does not understand the situation at your plant. After all, you have twenty-seven years' experience and you are much more competent than anyone else to make decisions affecting this plant. You know you will have to make your points *quickly* and *decisively* when you see him. He has to know who is boss at this location. Your prestige with your subordinate managers rests on the outcome of this meeting.

NOT-LISTENING ROLE-BRIEFING SHEET (Option No. 2)

Client

You have just moved into the city to begin a job with a small local business. On arriving two days ago, you were informed by this company that your position had to be dropped.

You are now unemployed, and your funds are running out. To make matters worse, your youngest child awoke this morning with a temperature of 103°. You called the company again, but all they could suggest was that you contact your Neighborhood Assistance Center.

You are about to talk to a case worker to get help. You are quite upset, and you feel you have no time to waste in small talk. You *must* make the case worker understand the seriousness of your situation. You feel that the staff member's sole concern should be to get you the help you need *immediately*.

Case Worker

You have been a case worker for two months at the Neighborhood Assistance Center. One of the biggest problems you face in your job is that most of the people you try to help have preset notions about what you should do for them.

You feel very strongly that the best solution to this problem is to inform a client precisely what services the Center does offer. Then he will be in a much better position to be helped.

Furthermore, you resent those clients who make demands rather than ask you for your help and advice. After all, you are the professional.

Therefore, at the beginning of any interview, you make sure that each client knows (1) that *you* are in a position to know what is best for helping *him* and (2) exactly what the various services of the Neighborhood Center are.

Structured Experience 52

53. BRAINSTORMING:
A PROBLEM-SOLVING ACTIVITY

Goals

I. To generate an extensive number of ideas or solutions to a problem by suspending criticism and evaluation.

II. To develop skills in creative problem-solving.

Group Size

Any number of small groups composed of approximately six participants each.

Time Required

Approximately one hour, for the described example.

Materials

Newsprint and felt-tipped marker for each group.

Physical Setting

Movable chairs for all participants.

Process

(The facilitator may wish to do the sample experience which follows as a preliminary to a problem-solving session involving a "real" problem.)

I. The facilitator forms small groups of approximately six participants each. Each group selects a secretary.

II. The facilitator instructs each group to form a circle. He provides newsprint and a felt-tipped marker for each secretary and asks him to record *every* idea generated by the group.

III. The facilitator states the following rules:

1. There will be no criticism during the brainstorming phase.

2. Far-fetched ideas are encouraged because they may trigger more practical ideas.

3. Many ideas are desirable.

IV. The facilitator announces that participants are to imagine being cast ashore on a desert island, nude and with nothing but a belt. *What can be done with the belt?* He tells the groups they have fifteen minutes to generate ideas.

V. At the end of the generating phase, the facilitator tells the groups that the ban on criticism is over. He directs them to evaluate their ideas and to select the best ones. (If there are four or more groups, the facilitator instructs two groups to share their best ideas and to form a single list.)

VI. The facilitator then asks participants to form one large group again. Secretaries act as spokesmen and take turns presenting the best ideas from their groups. Participants explore how two or more ideas might be used in combination.

VII. The facilitator writes the final list of ideas on newsprint, and the group is asked to rank-order them on the basis of feasibility.

VIII. The facilitator leads a discussion of brainstorming as an approach to creative problem-solving.

Variations

I. The exercise can be preceded by a loosening-up activity, such as playing with modeling clay.

II. Groups may be set up to compete with one another. Judges may be selected to determine criteria for ideas and to choose winning groups.

III. Other objects can be used in the problem. Participants may brainstorm uses for a flashlight, a rope, an oar, or a corkscrew. Props may be used.

Similar Structured Experiences: *Vol. II:* Structured Experience **31, 40;** *'73 Annual:* **91.**
Lecturette Source: *'73 Annual:* "Force-Field Analysis."

Structured Experience 53

Notes on the use of "Brainstorming":

54. TOWERS: AN INTERGROUP COMPETITION

Goals

    I. To study phenomena of competition among groups.

    II. To explore the feeling content and behavioral outcomes of winning and losing.

    III. To provide a basis for feedback to group members on their relations with other group members and their productivity in a task situation.

Group Size

Unlimited. (This is a multigroup exercise; each group should have no more than nine members.)

Time Required

Approximately one and one-half hours.

Materials

    I. Articles for auction: staplers, scissors, glue, string, and construction paper.

    II. Tower Judges' Role-Briefing Sheet for each group.

    III. Tower Observers' Role-Briefing Sheet for each group.

Physical Setting

A room large enough to permit several groups to work separately, but in sight of each other. For Process step I, each group should be seated separately as a group, facing one table on which all the articles for auction are displayed.

Process

    I. The facilitator briefly discusses goals of the activity and forms groups.

    II. Each group selects a representative to be on a panel of judges. These persons separate and form a group and then read the Tower Judges' Role-Briefing Sheet.

    III. An observer is selected for each group who goes away by himself to read the Tower Observers' Role-Briefing Sheet.

IV. The facilitator now auctions off the articles. He announces that each group has a sum of money—$100,000, for example. Each group selects a bidder. The facilitator announces a minimum bid for the first article, and the bidding begins.

V. He announces that each group is to build a construction-paper tower with its articles. One tower will be declared the winner, judged by the criteria of height, aesthetic appeal, and sturdiness.

VI. Each group constructs a tower with its articles. One observer takes notes on each group. There are no ground rules imposed on the tower-building process.

VII. When all groups are finished, the judges select a winning tower. The groups respond to the judgment. Each observer should note his group's reactions to the judging process and to the announcement of the winning tower.

VIII. Judges are asked to report on their experience. Each observer then reports on his group.

IX. The groups meet separately to process the exercise. Participants give each other feedback.

Variations

I. Instead of auctioning the articles, the facilitator can distribute them equally (or unequally) among the groups.

II. Judges and observers can be selected before the formation of groups, so that they do not "represent" groups.

III. The judges may distribute the articles in any manner *they* wish.

IV. Other criteria, such as cooperation, creativity, and speed, can be applied to determine the winning group.

V. The construction can be carried out nonverbally.

Similar Structured Experiences: *Vol. II:* Structured Experience **29, 32;** *'72 Annual:* **78, 81;** *Vol. IV:* **105.**
Lecturette Source: *'73 Annual:* "Win-Lose Situations."

Notes on the use of "Towers":

TOWER JUDGES' ROLE-BRIEFING SHEET

1. As a judge you will select a winning tower according to the criteria of height, aesthetic appeal, and sturdiness. You are *not* to evaluate the towers on other criteria, such as a group's cooperation.

2. You, the judges, will decide the relative weight given to the three criteria. You may or may not announce your weighting procedure.

3. You will decide whether your decision-making is to be public or private.

4. You should be fair in your judgment and not favor your group.

5. During the construction phase, you should function only as an observer.

Criterion	Judge	Group 1	2	3	4
Height	1				
	2				
(weight =)	3				
	4				
Aesthetic Appeal	1				
	2				
(weight =)	3				
	4				
Sturdiness	1				
	2				
(weight =)	3				
	4				

Winner: Group _____

TOWER OBSERVERS' ROLE-BRIEFING SHEET

1. You are to observe and record the significant behavior of your group and its individual members during the construction, judging, and reaction phases.

2. After the group's reactions to the judging, you will give a brief oral report of your observations.

3. Remember that feedback is more effective when it is specific, non-evaluative, focused on modifiable behavior, and checked to insure accuracy.

What the Group Did

During Construction:

During Judging:

Reacting to the Judging:

What Individuals Did

During Construction:

During Judging:

Reacting to the Judging:

55. GROUP SELF-EVALUATIONS: A COLLECTION OF INSTRUMENTS

Goals

I. To help a group evaluate its own functioning.

II. To provide a way to examine objectively the participation of group members.

III. To explore the norms that have developed in a group which has been meeting for some time.

Group Size

Eight to twelve members.

Time Required

Varies according to the evaluative procedures used.

Materials

I. Select one of the following forms and prepare copies of it for all participants:

Group-Climate Inventory.

Group-Growth Evaluation Form.

Feedback Rating Scales.

Postmeeting Reactions Form.

II. Pencils.

III. Newsprint and felt-tipped marker.

Physical Setting

Participants should be seated comfortably for writing, where they can see the posted results.

Process

Each of the following forms focuses on some aspect of group life which the facilitator may wish to discuss. A general process is suggested for the use of these inventories.

I. After a typical meeting of an ongoing group, the facilitator distributes copies of the form selected. Members are instructed to complete the form individually.

II. As soon as members finish, the data are posted on newsprint.

III. The facilitator leads a discussion of the data, eliciting specific instances of behavioral trends. He may offer appropriate theory material during this analytical stage.

IV. Group members are asked to plan new behavior for the next meeting in the light of the findings.

Variations

I. The facilitator may wish to use a different form at the end of each meeting in a sequence. Or the same form may be used several successive times, in order to study trends in the data; a group may thus chart its progress toward effective functioning.

II. Participants can predict the results of the analysis.

III. Forms may be modified to elicit expectations from new group members.

IV. Group members can collaborate on designing an instrument to measure the growth of the group.

Scoring Instructions: Group-Climate Inventory

Items 3, 6, 9, 12, and 16 are negative behaviors; they should be scored first: $A=0$, $T=1$, $U=2$, $S=3$, $R=4$, and $N=5$. All other items are scored the reverse: $A=5$, $T=4$, $U=3$, $S=2$, $R=1$, and $N=0$. The ratings in each of the four columns may then be added to obtain scores for each of the following aspects of group climate:

Column 1. Genuineness

Column 2. Understanding

Column 3. Valuing

Column 4. Acceptance

Similar Structured Experiences: *Vol. I:* Structured Experience 6; *Vol. II:* **39**; *'72 Annual:* **79**; *'73 Annual:* **92, 96**; *Vol. IV:* **113.**
Lecturette Sources: *'72 Annual:* "Openness, Collusion, and Feedback," "TORI Theory and Practice"; *'73 Annual:* "A Model of Group Development."

Structured Experience 55

Notes on the use of "Group Self-Evaluations":

GROUP-CLIMATE INVENTORY

Directions: Think about how your fellow group members as a whole normally behave toward you. Within the parentheses in front of the items below place the letter that corresponds to your perceptions of their behavior.

> A—They can *always* be counted on to behave this way.
>
> T—*Typically* I would expect them to behave this way.
>
> U—I would *usually* expect them to behave this way.
>
> S— They would *seldom* behave this way.
>
> R—They would *rarely* behave this way.
>
> N—I would *never* expect them to behave this way.

I Would Expect My Fellow Group Members To

1. (_____) level with me.
2. (_____) get the drift of what I am trying to say.
3. (_____) interrupt or ignore my comments.
4. (_____) accept me for what I am.
5. (_____) feel free to let me know when I "bug" them.
6. (_____) misconstrue things I say or do.
7. (_____) be interested in me.
8. (_____) provide an atmosphere in which I can be myself.
9. (_____) keep things to themselves to spare my feelings.
10. (_____) perceive what kind of person I really am.
11. (_____) include me in what's going on.
12. (_____) act "judgmental" with me.
13. (_____) be completely frank with me.
14. (_____) recognize when something is bothering me.
15. (_____) respect me, apart from my skills or status.
16. (_____) ridicule or disapprove of my peculiarities.

Structured Experience 55

GROUP-GROWTH EVALUATION FORM

Directions: Rate your group on each characteristic as the group was initially and as it is now. Use a seven-point scale with 7 as the highest rating.

Climate

Initially	Now	
_____	_____	1. I am treated as a human being, not as just another group member.
_____	_____	2. I feel close to the members of this group.
_____	_____	3. This group displays cooperation and teamwork.
_____	_____	4. Membership in this group is aiding my personal growth.
_____	_____	5. I have trust and confidence in the other members of this group.
_____	_____	6. Members of this group show supportive behavior toward each other.
_____	_____	7. I derive satisfaction from my membership in this group.
_____	_____	8. I feel psychologically close to this group.
_____	_____	9. I get a sense of accomplishment from my membership in this group.
	_____	10. I am being honest in responding to this evaluation.

Data Flow

Initially	Now	
_____	_____	11. I am willing to share information with other members of the group.
_____	_____	12. I feel free to discuss important personal matters with group members.

Goal Formation

Initially   **Now**

_____   _____   13. I am oriented toward personal goals rather than toward group objectives.

_____   _____   14. This group uses integrative, constructive methods in problem-solving, rather than a competitive approach.

_____   _____   15. I am able to deal promptly and well with the important problems of this group.

_____   _____   16. The activities of this group reflect a constructive integration of the needs and desires of its members.

_____   _____   17. My needs and desires are reflected in the activities of this group.

Control

Initially   **Now**

_____   _____   18. This group has a real sense of responsibility for getting a job done.

_____   _____   19. I feel manipulated by the group.

_____   _____   20. I think that I manipulate the group.

Structured Experience 55

FEEDBACK RATING SCALES

"Feedback" is a communication to a person (or a group) which gives that person information about how he affects others. Feedback helps an individual consider and alter his behavior and thus better achieve his goals.

Below are eight criteria for useful feedback. Rate the feedback that usually occurs in your group by circling the appropriate number on each of the eight scales. You also may want to make some notes for each criterion, such as particular group occurrences.

1. Useful feedback is *descriptive* rather than evaluative. It merely describes the sender's reaction, thus leaving the receiver free to use it or not. By avoiding evaluative language, it reduces the need for the receiver to respond defensively.

   Descriptive   1   2   3   4   5   6   **Evaluative**

   Comments:

2. It is *specific* rather than general. To be told that one is "dominating" will probably not be as useful as to be told: "Just now when we were deciding the issue, you did not listen to what others said, and I felt forced to accept your arguments or to face attack from you."

   Specific   1   2   3   4   5   6   **General**

   Comments:

3. It *takes into account the needs of both the receiver and the giver* of feedback. Feedback can be destructive when it serves only the giver's needs and fails to consider the needs of the receiver.

   Takes needs of both into account   1   2   3   4   5   6   **Does not take needs of both into account**

   Comments:

4. It is *directed toward behavior the receiver can change.* Frustration is only increased when one is reminded of a shortcoming over which he has no control.

   Directed towards modifiable behavior   1   2   3   4   5   6   **Directed towards nonmodifiable behavior**

   Comments:

5. It is *solicited* rather than imposed. Feedback is most useful when the receiver himself asks a question which those observing him can answer.

           Solicited   **1   2   3   4   5   6**   **Imposed**

Comments:

6. It is *well timed*. In general, feedback is most useful when given as soon as possible after the observed behavior (depending, of course, on the person's readiness to hear it, on support available from others, etc.).

           Well Timed   **1   2   3   4   5   6**   **Poorly Timed**

Comments:

7. It is *checked* with the sender. For example, the receiver can rephrase the feedback he has received to insure clear communication.

           Checked   **Not checked**
           with sender   **1   2   3   4   5   6**   **with sender**

Comments:

8. It is *checked with others* in the group. In a training group, particularly, both giver and receiver can check their feedback: Is it only one person's impression, or is it shared by others?

           Checked   **Not checked**
           with others   **1   2   3   4   5   6**   **with others**

Comments:

Adapted from theory session material contained in the *NTL 1968 Summer Reading Book*

Structured Experience 55

POSTMEETING REACTIONS FORM

Directions: You are to rank-order each statement in each set from 1 (most like) to 10 (least like) to describe the meeting and your behavior. Use this procedure: In each set, first identify the statement you would rank 1, then the one you would rank 10, then 2, then 9—alternating toward the middle of the scale.

The meeting was like this:

(   ) There was much warmth and friendliness.

(   ) There was much aggressive behavior.

(   ) People were uninterested and uninvolved.

(   ) People tried to dominate and take over.

(   ) We were in need of help.

(   ) Much of the conversation was irrelevant.

(   ) We were strictly task-oriented.

(   ) The members were very polite.

(   ) There was much underlying irritation.

(   ) We worked on our process issues.

My behavior was like this:

(   ) I was warm and friendly to some.

(   ) I did not participate much.

(   ) I concentrated on the job.

(   ) I tried to get everyone involved.

(   ) I took over the leadership.

(   ) I was polite to all.

(   ) My suggestions were frequently off the point.

(   ) I was a follower.

(   ) I was irritated.

(   ) I was eager and aggressive.

56. FEELINGS AND DEFENSES: A SPONTANEOUS LECTURE

Goals

I. To study feelings significant to group members and defenses they use.

II. To help group members take responsibility for their own learning.

Group Size

Unlimited.

Time Required

About thirty minutes.

Materials

Newsprint and felt-tipped markers.

Physical Setting

Members are seated in a semicircle.

Process

I. The facilitator briefly discusses goals. Then he instructs members to prepare a lecture on feelings and defenses. The planning is to be unstructured, except that someone is to take notes on newsprint.

II. Group members offer ideas about feelings and defenses. These are recorded.

III. The facilitator asks that someone volunteer to deliver the lecture. Then group members give him feedback.

IV. Subgroups are formed to process the experience. The facilitator may suggest that they consider their reactions to the planning, to the delivery, and to the content of the lecture.

Variations

    I. The topic can be changed. Some suggestions: risk-taking, openness, self-disclosure, intimacy, and dependency.

    II. Two or more volunteers can lecture through a team-teaching format.

    III. Subgroups can be formed to discuss points raised in step II.

    IV. A panel can be set up to discuss the subject. These persons may be coached by subgroups.

Similar Structured Experiences: *'72 Annual:* "Communication Modes: An Experiential Lecture"; *Vol. IV:* Structured Experience **104.**
Lecturette Sources: *'72 Annual:* "Defense Mechanisms in Groups"; *'73 Annual:* "Thinking and Feeling."

Notes on the use of "Feelings and Defenses":

57. NOMINATIONS: PERSONAL INSTRUMENTED FEEDBACK

Goals

I. To provide feedback to group members on how they are perceived by each other.

II. To analyze the climate and the norms of the group by studying members' behavior, composition of the group, and members' expectations of each other.

Group Size

Six to twelve members.

Time Required

Approximately one hour.

Materials

I. Select one of the following instruments and prepare copies for all participants:

Learning-Climate Analysis Form.

Group-Behavior Questionnaire.

Intentions and Choices Inventory.

II. Pencils.

Physical Setting

Participants should be seated so that they can write comfortably, preferably at tables or desk chairs.

Process

Each of the forms focuses on some aspect of group-member behavior which the facilitator may wish to discuss. This general process is suggested for each inventory.

I. The facilitator discusses goals and distributes copies of the form selected. Participants fill out the form individually.

II. As soon as members finish, they share their nominations of each other. (When the Learning-Climate Analysis Form is used, members also try to reach a consensus on each nomination.) Whenever possible, the person nominating specifies the incidents that led him to make that nomination.

III. The group members discuss the impact of the feedback on themselves.

IV. The group analyzes the effects of its members' behavior on the group. During this phase, the facilitator may wish to offer theories relating to climate, norms, and group composition.

V. Group members are urged to try, in later meetings, new behavior which reflects the results of this exercise.

Variations

I. Nominations can be posted on newsprint.

II. Participants can be asked to predict what nominations they will receive.

III. The group can devise its own nominations instrument.

IV. The same instrument can be used more than once during the "life" of the group.

Similar Structured Experiences: *Vol. I:* Structured Experience **13, 17, 18, 23**; *Vol. II:* **42**; *Vol. III:* **58**; *'72 Annual:* **79**; *'73 Annual:* **99**; *Vol. IV:* **104, 107.**
Lecturette Sources: *'72 Annual:* "Openness, Collusion, and Feedback"; *'73 Annual:* "Johari Window."

Notes on the use of "Nominations":

LEARNING-CLIMATE ANALYSIS FORM

Introduction: Learning about one's self, others, and groups is easier when group members feel free to be themselves; they contribute most to the group when they are most themselves, and they offer least when they are confined to one role.

People seem most free to be themselves when the level of trust in a group is high: Defensiveness is reduced, manipulative strategies tend to disappear, and the flow of information is increased. Instead, when the level of trust is low, people tend to be defensive, to adopt manipulative strategies, and to withhold information about themselves.

A high trust level seems to be encouraged when there is an increase in awareness, self-acceptance, acceptance of others, and problem-centering.

The purpose of this experience is to examine some of the dimensions of trust levels and to determine their effect on your group.

Instructions:

1. Read each definition.
2. Indicate which member you believe most closely resembles the description.
3. When everyone has finished, compare nominations for each of the dimensions.
4. Using the method of group consensus, select the one person who is most representative of each dimension.
5. Discuss what might be done to increase the trust level.

Definitions: A person may be said to be . . .

1. *Aware* when his outward behavior reflects his inner feelings and thoughts; when he explicitly recognizes how his feelings are influencing his behavior; when he recognizes and responds to feelings he experiences. Awareness may be indicated by a statement such as "I feel somewhat at a loss; we don't have a topic" (instead of "We're just floundering without something we can get our teeth into"). Or by "I'm not sure I want to say how I feel about you" (instead of "I don't think we ought to get personal").

   Your nomination_____ Consensus_____

2. *Self-accepting* when he is able to accept his own feelings without denying them, giving rationalizations for them, or apologizing for them. Self-acceptance may be evidenced by a statement such as "I'm bored with what you are saying" (instead of "This is a boring topic"). Or by "I'm angry at myself for being ineffective" (instead of "This group is not getting anywhere").

   Your nomination_____ Consensus_____

3. *Accepting of others* when he is able to accept the feelings and thoughts of others without trying to change them; when he is able to let others be themselves even though they are different from him. Acceptance of others may be shown by listening in order to understand; by listening without trying to refute; by trying not to argue; by asking questions in order to understand; or by not judging another.

   Your nomination_____ Consensus_____

4. *Supportive* when he seeks ways to help others reach goals that are important to them; when he tries to understand what others want to do, although he may not agree with their conclusions; or when he encourages others to try behavior new to them. Supportiveness may be seen in comments such as "Could you tell me how I might help you reach your objective" or "I am not sure I agree with what you are proposing, but I support your effort to get something going" or "Let me see if I understand what you want us to do."

   Your nomination_____ Consensus_____

Structured Experience 57

5. *Risk-taking* when he goes "beyond the known" by experimenting with new behavior; when he wants to accomplish something or to support someone else more than he wants to play it safe or to keep his cool; when he is willing to risk being angry, anxious, caring, driving, or retreating, even though these behaviors may make him appear foolish or inept or unintelligent or may arouse his anxiety. Risk-taking may be shown by initiating feedback on one's behavior or by supporting someone when it is not clear what the consequences will be or by giving feedback to others on their behavior.

Your nomination_____ Consensus_____

6. *Problem-centered* when he focuses on problems facing a group rather than on control or method; when he tries to learn by solving problems himself rather than by using someone else's solutions. Problem-centering may be seen in one's efforts to find out what is blocking a group, to increase personal effectiveness, and to probe beyond the symptoms. Problem-centering assumes that more work gets done when individuals and groups learn how to solve problems than when they maintain the same pattern of method, control, leadership, or feedback.

Your nomination_____ Consensus_____

7. *Leveling* when he is able to be open about his feelings and thoughts; when his outward behavior reflects his inner experience.

Your nomination_____ Consensus_____

GROUP-BEHAVIOR QUESTIONNAIRE

Instructions: Answer all questions with the *first names only* of two group members. Base your nominations on interactions in the group. Be sure to choose *two* people for each question. *Do not include yourself.*

1. Which members can most easily influence others to change their opinions?   _____   _____

2. Which are least able to influence others to change their opinions?   _____   _____

3. Which have clashed most sharply with others in the course of the meetings?   _____   _____

4. Which are most highly accepted by the group?   _____   _____

5. Which are most ready to support members?   _____   _____

6. Which try to keep themselves in the limelight?   _____   _____

7. Which are most likely to put personal goals above group goals?   _____   _____

8. Which have most often introduced topics not directly related to the group task?   _____   _____

9. Which have shown the greatest desire to accomplish something?   _____   _____

10. Which have wanted to avoid conflict in group discussions?   _____   _____

11. Which tend to withdraw from active discussion when strong differences begin to appear?   _____   _____

12. Which have sought to help in the resolution of differences between others?   _____   _____

13. Which have wanted the group to be warm, friendly, and comfortable?   _____   _____

14. Which have competed most with others?   _____   _____

15. Which have done most to keep the group lively?   _____   _____

16. Which would you choose to work with?   _____   _____

17. With which have you talked least?   _____   _____

Structured Experience 57

INTENTIONS AND CHOICES INVENTORY

Instructions: In the spaces below, put the names of the two individuals in your group who seem to fit best each of the descriptions. You may include yourself.

Intentions

1. He seems to be *aware* of his intentions and is able to communicate them without ambiguity; others are seldom in doubt about what his intentions are with respect to issues and group process.

    _____   _____

2. His intentions are *partially clear*, although there is some ambiguity; others are not always certain what this person intends with respect to issues and group process.

    _____   _____

3. His intentions are *derivable only by inference*; others can infer from his behavior what this person intends, but his intentions are not communicated.

    _____   _____

4. His intentions are *unclear*; others do not know where this person stands on issues or on group process.

    _____   _____

Choices

5. He seems to have a range of choices available in different situations; he does not simply react to outside signals but chooses his own path.

    _____   _____

6. He seems to want to make more choices but finds difficulty in doing much more than reacting.

    _____   _____

7. He seems to want others to make choices for him and for the group; he does not introduce his own preferences until he hears what a number of others say.

    _____   _____

8. He seems uncomfortable about making choices; he seems to prefer not to have to choose, and he is unhappy with situations in which he must do so.

    _____   _____

58. PEER PERCEPTIONS: A FEEDBACK EXPERIENCE

Goals

I. To let each group member know to what degree he is seen to be similar to each other member.

II. To study feeling reactions to being considered "different."

III. To help each member define the dimensions of human similarity and dissimilarity he believes are important.

Group Size

Eight to twelve members.

Time Required

Two to three hours.

Materials

I. Copies of the Peer Perceptions Ranking Form for all participants.

II. Copies of the Peer Perceptions Summary Form for all participants.

III. Pencils.

Physical Setting

Participants should be seated comfortably for writing.

Process

I. The facilitator explains goals.

II. Participants make certain they know the first names of everyone.

III. Participants are given the Peer Perceptions Ranking Form. Each participant is instructed to rank-order all participants, from the member he considers *most* similar to himself to the member he considers *least* similar. Beside each name, he lists the characteristics he had in mind.

IV. Peer Perceptions Summary Forms are distributed. The names of the group members should be listed in the *same order* in both vertical and horizontal columns on *all* the forms.

V. Each participant tells how he ranked members and what he had in mind when he made each ranking. Members record every ranking on the Summary Form and keep this form as a record. Each participant reacts to feedback he receives.

VI. The facilitator leads a discussion of the data, emphasizing how people react to being seen as "different" and how group members' values are expressed in the characteristics on which they focus.

Variations

I. Participants can rank-order each other on dimensions other than similarity. Examples: personal closeness, level of comfort, personal impact.

II. After step V, participants can be instructed to study their ranking forms to find recurring characteristics. These can be posted, to form the basis of a lecturette on projection and attribution.

III. Participants can be directed to predict the ranks they will receive.

IV. The ranking data can be collated by clerical assistants while the group is involved in another activity, such as a meal break.

Similar Structured Experiences: *Vol. I:* Structured Experience **13, 17, 18, 23;** *Vol. II:* **42;** *Vol. III:* **57;** *'72 Annual:* **79;** *'73 Annual:* **99;** *Vol. IV:* **104, 107.**
Lecturette Sources: *'72 Annual:* "Openness, Collusion, and Feedback"; *'73 Annual:* "Johari Window."

Submitted by John E. Jones, University Associates, San Diego, California.

Notes on the use of "Peer Perceptions":

PEER PERCEPTIONS RANKING FORM

| | *Your Ranking of Other Members* | *Characteristics Which You Considered* |

**Most
Similar
to You**

1._____   _____

2._____   _____

3._____   _____

4._____   _____

5._____   _____

6._____   _____

7._____   _____

8._____   _____

9._____   _____

10._____   _____

**Least
Similar
to You** 11._____   _____

PEER PERCEPTIONS SUMMARY FORM

Group Member Who Made Ranking

Group
Member
Ranked

	a	b	c	d	e	f	g	h	i	j	k	l
a												
b												
c												
d												
e												
f												
g												
h												
i												
j												
k												
l												

What Others Said About Me:

Structured Experience 58

59. LINE-UP AND POWER INVERSION: AN EXPERIMENT*

Goals

    I. To expand the individual's awareness of his influence on the group.

    II. To experience power inversion.

Group Size

    Eight to twelve participants.

Time Required

    Approximately one and one-half hours.

Materials

    I. Three sheets of paper and a pencil for each participant.

    II. Newsprint and a felt-tipped marker.

Physical Setting

    A room with ample space for the group to move around. Chairs arranged in a semicircle for phase 2.

Process

Phase 1:

    I. The facilitator instructs participants to arrange themselves in rank order according to each individual's influence on the group. This must be done nonverbally.

    II. Then the facilitator records the order on newsprint and posts it where it can be seen easily.

---

*This structured experience is best used in a design that links it with "Dividing the Loot," Structured Experience 60, following. "Line-Up and Power Inversion" should precede the use of "Dividing the Loot."

III. The group sits down and discusses the ranking experience. The facilitator may introduce certain observed behaviors, such as individuals withdrawing from the ranking process to avoid conflict.

IV. The facilitator asks the group to repeat the ranking process and the discussion as many times as necessary for the group to be satisfied that the rank order reflects each individual's influence.

Phase 2:

I. The facilitator tells the group that they are to elect an effective, "fair" leader. He explains that the voting power of each individual will be in inverse proportion to the amount of influence credited to that individual in the final rank order—*e.g.*, the member who ranked twelfth, or least influential, will have twelve votes, while the person ranked first will have just one vote. This will re-situate the power focus, allowing individuals to experiment with new behaviors involving power or lack of power.

II. The facilitator informs group members that they may caucus before this election but they may communicate only by written notes. They may have ten minutes to write notes. All notes will be delivered at the end of that time.

III. When notes have been delivered, the facilitator informs the group that the note-writing process may be repeated once or twice to complete the caucus.

IV. The group selects a leader by casting ballots. Ballots must show the rank-order number of the individual voting and the name of the individual for whom the ballot is cast. (Votes may *not* be split.)

V. The elected leader directs a group discussion on the impact of power refocusing. Afterwards, he solicits feedback on his leadership style.

Variations

I. Before the initial line-up, participants can independently rank-order group members according to influence (either influence on the group or on the participant himself).

II. Participants can be permitted to talk during the line-ups.

III. Other traits besides influence can be used. Participants can rank-order each other on openness, assertiveness, or congruence.

IV. The number of rounds in each phase can be varied.

Similar Structured Experiences: *Vol. III:* Structured Experience **58;** *Vol. IV:* **124.**

Structured Experience 59

Notes on the use of "Line-Up and Power Inversion":

60. DIVIDING THE LOOT: SYMBOLIC FEEDBACK*

Goals

I. To provide symbolic feedback to participants.

II. To explore the responsibilities and problems of leadership.

Group Size

Eight to twelve participants.

Time Required

One hour.

Materials

I. Money collected from the group members. (Each participant brings a specified amount, preferably in coins.)

II. Newsprint and felt-tipped marker.

Physical Setting

Chairs are placed in a circle.

Process

I. The facilitator instructs an elected leader to collect a specific sum, such as $2.00, from each group member. He then explains that the leader will reallocate this money on a criteria basis.

II. The facilitator indicates that the group will advise the leader in developing the criteria. The leader may wish to form subgroups to accomplish this. Criteria may include such factors as risk-taking, openness, helpfulness, or growth.

---

*This structured experience is best used in a design that links it with "Line-Up and Power Inversion," Structured Experience 59, preceding. "Dividing the Loot" should follow the use of "Line-Up and Power Inversion."

III. After suggestions have been made to the leader, he decides the actual criteria to be used. Ground rules:

    1. The money must be redistributed *unequally*.

    2. *No one* may receive the exact amount he contributed.

    3. Two or more criteria *must* be used.

    4. All the money must be redistributed to *individual participants*.

    5. The leader must include *himself* in the redistribution.

IV. The leader leaves the room for twenty minutes to work out the redistribution. While he is out, participants discuss what criteria would be most appropriate. Then each person predicts what he will receive and tells the others.

V. The leader returns, explains his selection of criteria, distributes the money, and processes the experience with the group. Discussion of behaviors, such as counterdependence and conflict avoidance, may be appropriate.

Variations

I. Other symbols such as medals or certificates can be used besides money.

II. A "steering committee" can be used instead of an elected leader. This committee could meet in the center of the room to redistribute the money.

III. The criteria can be established and applied by group consensus, with no elected leadership.

Similar Structured Experience: *Vol. I:* Structured Experience **23.**
Lecturette Sources: *'72 Annual:* "Openness, Collusion, and Feedback" and *'73 Annual:* "Risk-Taking."

Notes on the use of "Dividing the Loot":

61. PRISONERS' DILEMMA: AN INTERGROUP COMPETITION

Goals

    I. To explore trust between group members and effects of betrayal of trust.

    II. To demonstrate effects of interpersonal competition.

    III. To dramatize the merit of a collaborative posture in intragroup and intergroup relations.

Group Size

    Two teams of no more than eight members each.

Time Required

    Approximately one hour. (Smaller teams take less time.)

Materials

    I. Copies of the Prisoners' Dilemma Tally Sheet for all participants.

    II. Pencils.

Physical Setting

    Enough space for the two teams to meet separately without overhearing or disrupting each other. For step VII, two chairs for team representatives should be placed facing each other in the center of the room.

Process

    I. The facilitator explains that the group is going to experience a "risk-taking" situation similar to that experienced by guilty prisoners being interrogated by the police. Before interrogating prisoners suspected of working together, the questioner separates them and tells each one that the other has confessed and that, if they both confess, they will get off easier. The prisoners' dilemma or risk is that they may confess when they should not or they may fail to confess when they really should. (The facilitator carefully avoids discussing goals.)

    II. Two teams are formed and named Red and Blue. The teams are seated apart from each other. They are instructed not to communicate with the other team in any way, verbally or nonverbally, except when told to do so by the facilitator.

III. Prisoners' Dilemma Tally Sheets are distributed to all participants. They are given time to study the directions. The facilitator then asks if there are any questions concerning the scoring.

IV. Round 1 is begun. The facilitator tells the teams that they will have three minutes to make a team decision. He instructs them not to write their decisions until he signals them that time is up, so that they will not make hasty decisions.

V. The choices of the two teams are announced for Round 1. The scoring for that round is agreed upon and is entered on the scorecards.

VI. Rounds 2 and 3 are conducted in the same way as Round 1.

VII. Round 4 is announced as a special round, for which the payoff points are doubled. Each team is instructed to send one representative to the chairs in the center of the room. After representatives have conferred for three minutes, they return to their teams. Teams then have three minutes, as before, in which to make their decisions. When recording their scores, they should be reminded that points indicated by the payoff schedule are doubled for this round only.

VIII. Rounds 5 through 8 are conducted in the same manner as the first three rounds.

IX. Round 9 is announced as a special round, in which the payoff points are "squared" (multiplied by themselves: *e.g.*, a score of 4 would be $4^2 = 16$.) A minus sign should be retained: *e.g.*, $(-3)^2 = -9$. Team representatives meet for three minutes; then the teams meet for *five* minutes. At the facilitator's signal, the teams write their choices; then the two choices are announced.

X. Round 10 is handled exactly as Round 9 was. Payoff points are squared.

XI. The entire group meets to process the experience. The point total for each team is announced, and the sum of the two team totals is calculated and compared to the maximum positive or negative outcomes ($+126$ or -126 points). The facilitator may wish to lead a discussion about win-lose situations, zero-sum games, the relative merits of collaboration and competition, and the effects of high and low trust on interpersonal relations.

Variations

I. The competition can be carried out using money instead of points.

II. Process observers can be assigned to each team.

III. Teams can be placed in separate rooms, to minimize rule-breaking.

IV. The number of persons in each team can be varied.

V. In Round 10, each team can be directed to predict the choice of the other. These predictions can be posted before announcing the actual choices, as in the following diagram. (Actual choices are recorded in the circles after the predictions are announced.)

Predicting Team	Predicted Choice	
	Red Team	Blue Team
Red	◯	
Blue		◯

Similar Structured Experiences: *Vol. II:* Structured Experience **35, 36;** *'72 Annual:* **83.**
Lecturette Sources: *'72 Annual:* "Risk-Taking and Error Protection Styles"; *'73 Annual:* "Win-Lose Situations."

Notes on the use of "Prisoners' Dilemma":

PRISONERS' DILEMMA TALLY SHEET

Instructions: For ten successive rounds, the Red team will choose either an A or a B and the Blue Team will choose either an X or a Y. The score each team receives in a round is determined by the pattern made by the choices of both teams, according to the schedule below.

PAYOFF SCHEDULE

AX—Both teams win 3 points.
AY—Red Team loses 6 points; Blue Team wins 6 points.
BX—Red Team wins 6 points; Blue Team loses 6 points.
BY—Both teams lose 3 points.

SCORECARD

Round	Minutes	Choice		Cumulative Points	
		Red Team	Blue Team	Red Team	Blue Team
1	3				
2	3				
3	3				
4*	3 (reps.) 3 (teams)				
5	3				
6	3				
7	3				
8	3				
9**	3 (reps.) 5 (teams)				
10**	3 (reps.) 5 (teams)				

*Payoff points are doubled for this round.
**Payoff points are squared for this round. (Retain the minus sign.)

62. POLARIZATION: A DEMONSTRATION

Goals

I. To explore the experience of interpersonal polarization—its forms and effects.

II. To study conflict management and resolution.

Group Size

Twenty or more participants.

Time Required

Approximately two hours.

Materials

I. Copies of the Opinionnaire on Womanhood for all participants.

II. Pencils and paper.

III. Newsprint and felt-tipped marker.

Physical Setting

I. A room large enough to seat all participants.

II. Three adjacent rooms, each large enough to seat one-third of the participants.

III. For step VII, chairs arranged as described.

Process

I. The facilitator explains goals of the experience and stresses that participants should be honest and open.

II. Opinionnaires are distributed and are completed *individually* by participants. They are not to discuss their responses. The facilitator does not interpret items on the opinionnaire. If questions are asked, participants are urged simply to follow the directions.

III. When all participants have completed the opinionnaire, the facilitator announces the scoring scheme: Each "strongly agree" gets 2 points; each "agree" gets 1 point; each "uncertain" gets 0 points; each "disagree" gets –1 point; and each "strongly disagree" gets –2 points. He may wish to display the scoring scheme on newsprint.

SA	A	U	D	SD
2	1	0	–1	–2

After all participants have computed their scores, the facilitator asks each person to add 30 points to his score, to eliminate negative scores.

IV. A tally of the scores is made on newsprint, using the following format:

Score Interval	Number of Scores
55-60	_____
50-54	_____
45-49	_____
40-44	_____
35-39	_____
30-34	_____
25-29	_____
20-24	_____
15-19	_____
10-14	_____
5-9	_____
0-4	_____
Number of Participants: _____	

V. On the basis of their scores (high, middle, and low), participants are divided into three groups of roughly equal size. (It may be necessary to get individual scores for the high and low intervals in the middle group.)

VI. The three groups are sent to separate rooms for about twenty minutes. Each should select a spokesman, achieve consensus on a point of view about modern womanhood, and instruct its spokesman on a strategy for persuading the other groups to accept its position.

VII. All participants are brought back into the large room, which has been arranged in such a way that the three groups sit apart from each other. The three spokesmen sit facing each other in the center of the room. They discuss their opinions for approximately fifteen minutes.

VIII. The three groups recaucus for about fifteen minutes in their separate rooms with their spokesmen. Each spokesman receives feedback, further instructions, and suggestions.

IX. The entire group reassembles as before. The facilitator announces that, after about fifteen minutes of further exchange among the spokesmen, the middle group will vote for the position of either the high or the low group. The spokesmen then discuss their viewpoints.

X. The facilitator distributes paper for ballots to all members of the middle group, who vote individually for either "high" or "low." The ballots are collected. (This is a good point for a coffee break.) The votes are announced one at a time. Members are encouraged to give reasons why they voted as they did.

XI. The facilitator leads a general discussion of the exercise, eliciting comments on what polarization feels like, what its effects are, and how to deal with interpersonal conflict.

Variations

I. Within the caucuses, participants can form subgroups on particular opinionnaire items.

II. New spokesmen can be selected for the second meeting of spokesmen.

III. Groups can be instructed to display their major points on newsprint.

IV. Groups of unequal sizes can be established. Ordinarily, the middle group should be the largest.

Similar Structured Experience: *Vol. III:* Structured Experience **68.**
Lecturette Source: *'73 Annual:* "Confrontation: Types, Conditions, and Outcomes."

Submitted by John E. Jones, University Associates, San Diego, California, and Johanna J. Jones, University of Iowa, Iowa City, Iowa.

Structured Experience 62

Notes on the use of "Polarization":

POLARIZATION: OPINIONNAIRE ON WOMANHOOD

Instructions: In front of each statement, place one of the abbreviations from the list below to indicate the extent to which you agree or disagree with the statement.

> SA—Strongly Agree
> A—Agree
> U—Uncertain
> D—Disagree
> SD—Strongly Disagree

_____ 1. Women should have the right to abortion on demand.

_____ 2. Free day care for children is a right which all women should be able to demand.

_____ 3. Marriage is an institution that benefits males primarily.

_____ 4. Today's divorce laws are demeaning to women.

_____ 5. Employment practices in the U.S. discriminate against women.

_____ 6. The use of female sex appeal in advertising should be stopped.

_____ 7. Job vacancy notices should not mention sex.

_____ 8. Women should receive equal pay for equal work.

_____ 9. Women should receive preferential treatment right now as indemnity for past discrimination.

_____ 10. Women, because of their sensitivity, are superior to men in all work that does not rely primarily on brute strength.

_____ 11. Women should not be barred from careers because they are mothers.

_____ 12. The charge that women are overly emotional is a male "smoke screen."

_____ 13. Women are under-represented in public office.

_____ 14. A woman should be able to have herself sterilized without her husband's permission.

_____ 15. Birth control information and devices should be available to any female over fourteen who requests them.

Structured Experience 62

63. DISCRIMINATION: SIMULATION ACTIVITIES

Each of the following experiences is designed to explore interpersonal stereotyping and discrimination.

1. By any arbitrary procedure, a "minority" group is selected and is required to wear black masks during a group meeting. Masked members are instructed to follow rather than to lead, to address others as "sir" and "ma'am," and to "think Black." Nonmasked members may address them as "boy," "girl," and "you people." Members later explore the effects of the masks and the ways racial discrimination is experienced and reinforced.

2. A group that consists of less than half of the participants is selected and asked to wear bead necklaces for the duration of the event. This group is instructed to sit together at meals. Toward the end of the event, a meeting is held to process the experience of designating a minority as "different."

3. Participants count off "black, white, black, white, black, white," etc. "Blacks" are asked to leave the room. "Whites" stay, take off their shoes, and pile them in the center of the floor. "Blacks" are asked to return, match shoes, find the owner of a pair, and put them on the owner's feet—all without speaking. The two groups meet separately to share their observations and feeling reactions. There is then a general discussion.

Similar Structured Experiences: *Vol. II:* Structured Experience **41;** *Vol. IV:* **124.**
Lecturette Sources: *'73 Annual:* "A Transactional Analysis Primer," "Some Implications of Value Clarification for Organization Development."

Notes on the use of "Discrimination":

64. KERNER REPORT:
A CONSENSUS-SEEKING TASK

Goals

I. To compare the results of individual decision-making with the results of group decision-making.

II. To generate data to discuss decision-making patterns in task groups.

III. To diagnose the level of development in a task group.

Group Size

Between five and twelve participants. Several groups may be directed simultaneously in the same room. (Synergistic outcomes are more likely to be achieved by smaller groups, *i.e.*, five to seven participants.)

Time Required

Approximately one hour.

Materials

I. Copies of the Kerner Report Worksheet for all participants.

II. Pencils.

III. Newsprint and felt-tipped marker.

Physical Setting

Participants should be seated around a square or a round table, as a rectangular table gives too much control to persons seated at the ends. Lapboards may be provided for participants seated in a circle.

Process

I. The facilitator explains goals. Each participant is given a copy of the worksheet. The task is to rank-order the items according to the instructions on the form. (It is usually desirable for the facilitator to read the instructions aloud). Participants are to work *individually* during this phase, which should take no more than ten minutes.

II. Groups are formed and asked to derive a ranking of the items by consensus. There must be *substantial agreement* (not necessarily unanimity) on the rank assigned. Three ground rules are imposed in this phase:

   1. No averaging.

   2. No "majority-rule" voting.

   3. No "horse-trading."

Suggestions about how consensus can be achieved:

   1. Members should avoid arguing in an attempt to win as individuals. What is "right" is the best collective judgment of the group as a whole.

   2. Conflict about ideas, solutions, predictions, etc. should be viewed as helping rather than hindering consensus.

   3. Problems are solved best when individual group members accept responsibility for both listening and contributing, so that everyone is included in the decision.

   4. Tension-reducing behaviors can be useful if meaningful conflict is not "smoothed over" prematurely.

   5. Each member is responsible for monitoring the processes through which work gets done and for initiating discussions of process when work is becoming ineffective.

   6. The best results flow from a fusion of information, logic, and emotion. Value judgments include members' feelings about the data and about the process of decision-making.

The facilitator should stress that the groups must work hard to be successful. This phase should take about thirty minutes.

III. The "right" answers are read aloud or can be posted by the facilitator. The score is the sum of the differences between what the correct rank is for each item and how it was ranked in the exercise. (All differences should be made positive and added together.) Participants are directed to derive the following statistics for each group: the range of individual scores, the average of individual scores, the score for group consensus, and the difference between the average and the group consensus score.

IV. The group computes the average score of the individual members, compares this with the group's score, and discusses the implications of the experience. This processing might be focused on leadership, compromise decision-making strategies, the feeling content of the exercise, the roles played by members, or other aspects of group life.

Structured Experience 64

The goal is to rank grievances under three levels of intensity. It is necessary to place each grievance in the exact order as in the actual report. (A new answer key can be established by conducting a survey of a relevant referent group.)

Answer Key:

First Level of Intensity

1. __D__ Police practices.

2. __J__ Unemployment and underemployment.

3. __E__ Inadequate housing.

Second Level of Intensity

4. __H__ Inadequate education.

5. __C__ Poor recreation facilities and programs.

6. __K__ Ineffective political structure and grievance mechanisms.

Third Level of Intensity

7. __B__ Disrespectful White attitudes.

8. __F__ Discriminatory administration of justice.

9. __I__ Inadequate federal programs.

10. __L__ Inadequate municipal services.

11. __A__ Discriminatory consumer and credit practices.

12. __G__ Inadequate welfare programs.

Variations

I. Ranking forms can be developed both before the training session and during the event. For example, a list of top problems facing the group involved can be written. This list can be rank-ordered by a random sample of members of the group, and their responses can be tallied to develop an answer key. Also, within the training session, a list of items can be developed by participants for a ranking task. A survey of all participants can be conducted to develop a set of "right" answers.

II. Groups can be encouraged to experiment with alternatives to formal voting procedures: They can seat themselves in the order that they ranked a given item as individuals; they can rate their agreement with each item; or they can distribute points among alternatives.

III. The group-on-group design (*Vol. I*: Structured Experience 6) can be used to heighten participation in consensus-seeking. Two rounds can be used, with two different ranking tasks.

IV. The facilitator can experiment with various group sizes. Participants can be assigned randomly to groups and the groups given a time limit for consensus-seeking. They can rate their satisfaction with the outcomes before the scoring. Groups' average satisfaction ratings can be compared to other statistical outcomes.

V. Similar experiments can be devised to vary time limits for consensus-seeking. For example, one group can be given twenty minutes, another thirty minutes, and one unlimited time. Satisfaction data and outcomes can be compared. (A more complex design would be to study the effects of group size and time limit simultaneously, as in the following model which requires nine groups.)

	Group Size		
Time	Small	Medium	Large
Brief			
Long			
No Limit			

VI. As an intergroup task, the same ranking form can be filled out by two groups. Then each group can be instructed to predict the ranking of the other group. The two groups can be brought together to publish their actual rankings and sets of predictions. This activity gives each group a "mirror image" of itself and can lead to more effective communication between groups.

VII. Participants can be asked to rank-order each other (independently) in terms of the amount of influence each had on the consensus-seeking outcomes. Then each participant derives a score for himself based on the differences between his ranking of the items and the consensus ranking. The average influence ranks and the deviation scores are then correlated.

VIII. Sequential consensus exercises can be used, so that groups build on what was learned in the first phase. New groups can be formed for the second round. One task may have "right" answers, and the other may not. The group may create its own instrument for the second phase.

Structured Experience 64

IX. The facilitator can save considerable group time and often considerable confusion by handing out two copies of the exercise form to each participant. The participant fills in both copies along with his group identification number before his group begins its discussion. He hands one copy to the facilitator and keeps the other for his group-consensus discussion. While the group is involved in developing a consensus ranking, the facilitator may find each group's range of individual scores and average of individual scores. This task goes most quickly if there are several staff members. A chart of all results may be developed and shared with all participants when the groups have finished their processing.

Similar Structured Experiences: *Vol. I:* Structured Experience **11;** *Vol. II:* **30;** *Vol. III:* **69;** *'72 Annual:* **77;** *Vol. IV:* **115.**
Lecturette Source: *'73 Annual:* "Synergy and Consensus-Seeking."

Notes on the use of "Kerner Report":

KERNER REPORT WORKSHEET

Introduction: In gathering data on twenty-four disorders in twenty-three cities, the U.S. Riot Commission Report (Kerner Report) found that "Although specific grievances varied from city to city, at least twelve deeply held grievances can be identified and ranked into three levels of relative intensity."

Instructions: You are part of an evaluating team for the U.S. Riot Commission. Among the data gathered are twelve basic grievances of Blacks involved in the rioting. Having reviewed all the data, you choose to rank the grievances under three levels of intensity, the first being the highest.

List of grievances to be ranked under the three levels:

    A. Discriminatory consumer and credit practices

    B. Disrespectful White attitudes

    C. Poor recreation facilities and programs

    D. Police practices

    E. Inadequate housing

    F. Discriminatory administration of justice

    G. Inadequate welfare programs

    H. Inadequate education

    I.   Inadequate federal programs

    J.   Unemployment and underemployment

    K. Ineffective political structure and grievance mechanisms

    L. Inadequate municipal services

First Level of Intensity		Second Level of Intensity		Third Level of Intensity	
You	*Your Group*	*You*	*Your Group*	*You*	*Your Group*
1. ( )	( )	4. ( )	( )	7. ( )	( )
2. ( )	( )	5. ( )	( )	8. ( )	( )
3. ( )	( )	6. ( )	( )	9. ( )	( )
				10. ( )	( )
				11. ( )	( )
				12. ( )	( )

Structured Experience 64

65. THINK-FEEL: A VERBAL PROGRESSION

Goals

    I. To make distinctions between thoughts and feelings.

    II. To learn to link feeling feedback to observable behavior.

    III. To practice empathizing.

Group Size

Unlimited number of groups of three to five members each.

Time Required

Forty-five minutes.

Materials

Newsprint and felt-tipped marker.

Physical Setting

A room large enough to permit each small group to interact verbally without disturbing other groups.

Process

    I. The facilitator discusses goals. Then he forms small groups. (Count the number of participants and divide by 3, 4, or 5 to determine the number of groups. Have participants count off by this number to form relatively heterogeneous groups.)

    II. The facilitator explains that there will be four rounds of communication and that he will be interrupting each round as necessary. A few minutes of processing within the small groups follows each round.

    III. *Round 1.* The facilitator writes on newsprint the phrase "Now I see." He tells participants to describe the nonverbal behavior of the other members of their group by statements that begin with the phrase "Now I see." He illustrates briefly by describing the movements of some nearby participants. Round 1 takes five minutes. The facilitator may have to interrupt if participants begin to move away from behavior description toward discussion. The round should be followed by about two minutes for processing.

70

IV. *Round 2.* The facilitator writes the phrase "Now I think" and instructs participants to continue their conversation by beginning each sentence with the phrase "Now I think." He may wish to give an example. Round 2 takes five minutes, followed by two minutes for processing.

V. *Round 3.* The third phrase is "Now I feel." After about two minutes of interaction, the facilitator interrupts to explain that groups that focus on feeling data commonly confuse thoughts and feelings. He suggests that members avoid the following two phrases in the remainder of this round:

> I feel that . . .
>
> I feel like . . .

Instead, members are to use the phrase "Now I feel," followed by an *adjective*. They should be mindful of the tendency to center their attention on the other person rather than to express their own feelings. Round 3 takes about ten minutes, followed by about three minutes for processing.

VI. *Round 4.* The facilitator posts the fourth phrase, "Now I think you feel," which participants are to use to begin each of their communications to other members. Since this round focuses on empathic understanding, conversations should be two-way, to determine the accuracy of the members' perceptions of each other's feelings. Round 4 takes ten minutes, followed by three minutes of processing.

VII. *Total Group Processing.* The facilitator leads a discussion of the results of the experience, focusing on the learning goals specified.

Variations

I. The activity can be carried out in dyads.

II. The timing of each round can be varied from that described.

III. The activity can be "staged" in front of the group as a demonstration.

Similar Structured Experiences: *Vol. III:* Structured Experience **50, 56;** *Vol. IV:* **106.**
Lecturette Sources: *'72 Annual:* "Communication Modes: An Experiential Lecture"; *'73 Annual:* "Thinking and Feeling."

Submitted by John E. Jones, University Associates, San Diego, California.

Structured Experience 65

Notes on the use of "Think-Feel":

66. TEAM-BUILDING:
A FEEDBACK EXPERIENCE

Goals

   I. To help an intact work group diagnose its functioning.

   II. To establish a cooperative expectation within a task group.

   III. To assist a "real-life" group or business manager (leader, chairman, supervisor) to develop norms of openness, trust, and interdependence among team members and/or members of his organization.

   IV. To help team members clarify and evaluate their personal goals, the team's goals, and the relationship between these two sets of aims.

Group Size

No more than twelve members.

Time Required

A minimum of one day. (The time required varies according to the depth of the intervention. The example described here requires three days.)

Materials

   I. Sensing Interview Guide.

   II. Newsprint and felt-tipped marker.

Physical Setting

A private room with wall space for posting.

Process

   I. *Phase 1: Sensing.* Prior to the team-building meeting, the facilitator interviews each of the team members privately. He indicates to each what his purposes are, what the limits of confidentiality are, and what he is going to do with the interview data. The Sensing Interview Guide may be used and/or adapted in preparation for these interviews. (See *'73 Annual:* "The Sensing Interview.")

II. *Phase 2: Data Analysis.* The interview data are analyzed by the facilitator. He notes common themes running through the responses of team members. He prepares a series of posters from the data: a poster of data pertaining to each team member, a poster containing data on the group's process (decision-making patterns, communication phenomena, etc.), a poster displaying goal statements, a poster of team-building meeting objectives, and a poster representing any other groupings of data which emerge from his analysis.

III. *Phase 3: Team-Building.* The team assembles in a room that has a minimum of outside interruptions. The facilitator explains the goals of the two-day meeting, and he posts his objectives. Then he posts all the rest of the interview data, explaining his analysis. (He may wish to display his posters one at a time, entertaining clarifying questions on each.) He spends the rest of the meeting facilitating the team's working on the posted data—reinforcing openness, risk-taking, trust, and interdependence. He may suggest a confrontation between the manager and the rest of the members, but he is careful to help the manager learn how to give and receive feedback nondefensively. The facilitator helps the team members learn how to observe group process. Decisions made by the group are written on newsprint and posted. The facilitator may urge members to develop contracts with each other for follow-up.

Variations

I. A variation on the sensing strategy described in phase 1 is the *sensing meeting*. The manager calls a meeting to gather data on his part of the organization. He chairs the meeting—soliciting data and writing them on newsprint. The facilitator helps the manager listen, avoid reacting defensively, and record the data. The manager then commits himself to a definite course of action in dealing with the data. These meetings may consist of the manager and his immediate assistants, or they may include vertical, horizontal, or diagonal slices of his organization. All subordinates who joined the organization within the last year, for example, may be able to point out flaws in the structure.

II. The analysis can be carried out with the assistance of a colleague and/or the manager. (The facilitator needs to be sensitive to the credibility of the outcomes, however.)

III. Instead of posters, the facilitator can distribute copies of his analysis to each member of the team.

Similar Structured Experiences: *Vol. III:* Structured Experience 55; *Vol. IV:* **118.**
Lecturette Sources: *'72 Annual:* "An Introduction to Organization Development," "Notes on Freedom"; *'73 Annual:* "Planned Renegotiation—A Norm-Setting OD Intervention," "The Sensing Interview," "An Informal Glossary of Terms and Phrases in Organization Development."

Notes on the use of "Team-Building":

TEAM-BUILDING: SENSING INTERVIEW GUIDE

Name _____ Interviewer_____

Date _____ Time_____to _____

Format: Face to Face _____(or) By Phone_____Place _____

  1. Title(s) of interviewee _____

  2. Relation to the team _____

  _____

  3. Satisfaction with team's current functioning_____

  _____

  4. Goals of the team _____

  _____

  5. Personal goals_____

  _____

  _____

  6. How decisions are made_____

  _____

  7. Problems of the team right now _____

  _____

  _____

  8. Personal problems related to the team right now _____

  _____

  _____

  9. Action strategies needed right now _____

  _____

10. Feelings about the team-building meeting _____

  _____

  _____

11. Relationships with other team members (give first names and titles—*e.g.*, manager/leader/chairman/supervisor)

A._____ _____

B._____ _____

C._____ _____

D._____ _____

E._____ _____

F._____ _____

G._____ _____

H._____ _____

I._____ _____

J._____ _____

K._____ _____

L._____ _____

12. Other comments_____

_____

Structured Experience 66

67. ORGANIZATIONAL MIRROR: A FEEDBACK EXPERIENCE

Goals

I. To generate data that can permit an organization (department, team, club, staff, etc.) to diagnose its functioning.

II. To establish avenues of feedback between an organization and other groups with which it is linked—departments, customers, etc.

Group Size

Varies.

Time Required

Approximately two hours.

Materials

Newsprint, a felt-tipped marker, and masking tape.

Physical Setting

A room without tables, large enough to hold the key members of the organization and invited representatives. Adequate wall space for posting newsprint sheets.

Process

I. In advance of the "mirroring" meeting, the facilitator helps the organization decide which outsiders are to be invited and how they are to be oriented. The organization asks these representatives to come to the meeting.

II. The leader of the organization conducts the meeting, while the facilitator tries to keep members of the organization nondefensive and to help them listen to the feedback. A member of the organization takes notes on newsprint and posts the data as generated. Outside representatives are encouraged to be open and specific in giving feedback; the chairman assures them that the purpose of the meeting is to help his organization improve its effectiveness.

III. Members of the organization discuss their plans for the data and contract to follow through with the invited representatives. The facilitator helps members focus on processing the data rather than on responding to the feedback.

IV. After the meeting, the facilitator gives feedback to the chairman on his conduct of the meeting.

Variations

I. After receiving feedback, the group can assemble in the center of the room for initial reactions. This meeting can be interrupted for the group to receive additional feedback on its process.

II. A follow-up meeting can be announced as a part of the invitation to the organizational mirror meeting.

III. The facilitator can interview representative outsiders instead of inviting them to attend a meeting.

IV. The organization can survey individuals in other organizations with which it is linked.

Similar Structured Experience: *Vol. III:* Structured Experience **68.**
Lecturette Sources: *'72 Annual:* "An Introduction to Organization Development," "Notes on Freedom"; *'73 Annual:* "Planned Renegotiation—A Norm-Setting OD Intervention," "The Sensing Interview," "An Informal Glossary of Terms and Phrases in Organization Development."

Notes on the use of "Organizational Mirror":

68. INTERGROUP MEETING: AN IMAGE EXCHANGE

Goals

    I. To improve the relationship between two groups, such as levels of management, majority-minority groups, males and females.

    II. To explore how groups interact with each other.

Group Size

    Two groups of not more than twelve participants each.

Time Required

    Three hours.

Materials

    Newsprint, felt-tipped markers, and masking tape.

Physical Setting

    One room large enough to seat the members of both groups and with wall space for posting newsprint sheets. Two nearby rooms, each large enough to accommodate one of the groups.

Process

    I. In a general meeting, the facilitator discusses goals and the schedule of events.

    II. Groups meet separately for one hour to generate two sets of data on the sheets of newsprint: (1) how they see the other group and (2) how they think the other group sees them.

    III. The total group reassembles, and spokesmen for the two groups post and explain the data. During this phase, the facilitator helps members listen, but not respond, to the feedback. Their goal is to understand the perceptions of the other group. This phase takes thirty minutes.

    IV. The two groups meet separately again for one hour to respond to the data and to plan how to process it.

V. In a third general meeting of thirty minutes, members of the two groups share their reactions to the feedback. Discussion leads to diagnosis of the way the two groups are interacting. Members make contracts across groups to follow through after the meeting.

Variations

I. Individual team members can be asked to write down their perceptions before the group meetings.

II. Groups can direct their attention to critical incidents in the history of the relationship between the two groups. They may be restricted to a list of adjectives only as feedback.

III. The process can be carried out in a series of meetings over a period of days or weeks.

Similar Structured Experience: *Vol. III:* Structured Experience **67.**
Lecturette Sources: *'72 Annual:* "An Introduction to Organization Development," "Notes on Freedom"; *'73 Annual:* "Planned Renegotiation—A Norm-Setting OD Intervention," "The Sensing Interview," "An Informal Glossary of Terms and Phrases in Organization Development."

Notes on the use of "Intergroup Meeting":

69. SUPERVISORY BEHAVIOR/AIMS OF EDUCATION: CONSENSUS-SEEKING TASKS

Goals

I. To explore the relationships between subjective involvement with issues and problem-solving.

II. To teach effective consensus-seeking behaviors in task groups.

Group Size

Ten or more participants. (In the example described here, two subgroups of five members each are established.)

Time Required

Approximately one and one-half hours.

Materials

I. Copies of the Supervisory Behavior Worksheet for members of the inner-circle subgroup (see step III).

II. Copies of the Aims of Education Worksheet for members of the second inner-circle subgroup (see step VII).

III. Pencils.

Physical Setting

Movable chairs which can be arranged in a group-on-group design. (See *Vol. I: Structured Experience 6.*)

Process

I. The facilitator divides the group into two subgroups and instructs participants of one group to choose a "partner" from the other group.

II. He arranges the subgroups in concentric circles, facing the center, and explains that the outer-circle group will act as personal process observers; they will give feedback to their "partners" in the inner-circle group following the first group ranking session. He adds that a second ranking session will be held in which the roles of the two groups will be reversed and that new partners will be chosen for that session.

III. Copies of the Supervisory Behavior Worksheet are given to all participants in the inner circle. The facilitator explains that the inner circle is to work as a group in discussing and ranking the statements on their sheets. The group must *not* choose a formal discussion leader. It may arrive at its decisions by any method. As the group makes a decision, participants are to record the group ranking for each statement on the worksheet. They are to place the number 1 within the parentheses in front of the statement considered to be the most important characteristic of effective supervisory behavior and so on through number 8, the least important characteristic.

IV. The facilitator reminds the personal process observers of their roles in observing their partners.

V. He tells the inner-circle group that it has twenty minutes to complete the ranking and cautions members that they may not complete their task in that amount of time.

VI. At the end of twenty minutes, the facilitator directs personal process observers to give their "partners" feedback privately for ten minutes.

VII. New partners are chosen. The process is repeated, with the outer circle becoming the inner circle and the inner group acting as personal process observers. During this phase, Aims of Education Worksheets are used by the inner circle.

VIII. When the process is finished, the facilitator may wish to give a brief lecture on task versus process.

IX. The facilitator leads a discussion of the experience.

Variations

See "Kerner Report: A Consensus-Seeking Task," Structured Experience 64, on page 64.

Similar Structured Experiences: *Vol. I:* Structured Experience **6, 11;** *Vol. II:* **30;** *Vol. III:* **64;** *'72 Annual:* **77, 79;** *'73 Annual;* **92;** *Vol. IV:* **115.**
Lecturette Sources: *'73 Annual:* "Synergy and Consensus-Seeking," "The Hill Interaction Matrix (HIM) Conceptual Framework for Understanding Groups."

The worksheets are adapted from *Handbook of Staff Development and Human Relations Training: Materials Developed for Use in Africa* by Donald Nylen, J. Robert Mitchell, and Anthony Stout. They are used with permission of the National Training Laboratories Institute for Applied Behavioral Science.

Structured Experience 69

Notes on the use of "Supervisory Behavior/Aims of Education":

SUPERVISORY BEHAVIOR WORKSHEET

Instructions:

1. You *must* work as a group.
2. Do *not* choose a formal discussion leader.
3. Record the ranking as the group decides upon it.

(_____) He freely praises excellent work.

(_____) He communicates his reasons for all important decisions to his subordinates.

(_____) He encourages criticism of his policies by his subordinates.

(_____) He consults with his subordinates before making decisions affecting their work.

(_____) He has no favorites.

(_____) He never reprimands a subordinate in front of others.

(_____) He has frequent social contacts with his subordinates while off the job.

(_____) He delegates authority to his subordinates on all matters directly affecting their work.

Structured Experience 69

AIMS OF EDUCATION WORKSHEET

Instructions:

1. You *must* work as a group.
2. Do *not* choose a formal discussion leader.
3. Record the ranking as the group decides upon it.

(_____) Society is held together by proper behavior. Education should teach people to be good, honest, upright human beings.

(_____) People are happiest when they know they have done a skillful job. Therefore, they should be taught things that will help them do their work better.

(_____) Knowledge should be valued for its own sake, because in knowledge there is wisdom. Education should teach those things that have been found to be true for all people for all times.

(_____) The family is most important. Education should teach one to be a more able and responsible family member.

(_____) In these times, when we must all work together to build our country, education must first teach us to be informed, reliable, and cooperative citizens.

(_____) It is natural for people to want a reasonably comfortable way of life and a share in the good things of life. Education should primarily teach people how to attain money and success.

(_____) If our nation is to go forward, our people must know and understand their own historical and cultural roots. Education should teach us about our past and how it can help or hinder us today.

(_____) Freedom means choice. An uneducated person may believe all or nothing of what he hears or reads. Education should teach people how to make intelligent choices in all areas of their lives.

70. INTIMACY PROGRAM: DEVELOPING PERSONAL RELATIONSHIPS

Goals

I. To accelerate the getting-acquainted process in groups.

II. To study the experience of self-disclosure.

III. To develop authenticity in groups.

Group Size

Unlimited.

Time Required

Approximately one and one-half hours.

Materials

Copies of the Intimacy Program Guidelines for all participants.

Physical Setting

A room large enough for dyads to talk privately without disturbing each other.

Process

I. The facilitator introduces the program with a brief lecture on self-disclosure and the building of trust. He explains the goals of the program.

II. Group members pair off, preferably with people whom they know least well.

III. The Intimacy Program is described, the ground rules are explained, and the Guidelines are distributed.

IV. Pairs meet for approximately one hour.

V. Groups of three or four dyads are formed to process the experience.

VI. The total group hears reports from each of the small groups.

Variations

I. Larger groups than dyads can be used.

II. The Guidelines can be augmented by questions suggested by participants.

III. Participants can develop their own guidelines. Each person can be instructed to write down an "intimate" question; the questions are then collected, collated, and reproduced.

IV. The program can be carried out between people who already know each other.

Similar Structured Experiences: *Vol. I:* Structured Experience **18, 21;** *Vol. II:* **45;** *'73 Annual:* **87;** *Vol. IV:* **116, 118.**
Lecturette Sources: *'72 Annual:* "Openness, Collusion, and Feedback"; *'73 Annual:* "Johari Window," "Risk-Taking," "Dependency and Intimacy."

The guidelines were adapted from S.D. Jourard, *Disclosing Man to Himself* (Princeton, N.J.: Van Nostrand, 1968).

Notes on the use of "Intimacy Program":

INTIMACY PROGRAM GUIDELINES

Instructions: During the time allotted for this experience you are to ask questions from this list. The questions vary in their degree of intimacy, and you may want to begin with less intimate ones. Take turns initiating the questions. Follow the rules below.

1. Your communication with your partner will be held in confidence.

2. You must be willing to answer any question that you ask your partner.

3. You may decline to answer any question initiated by your partner.

How important is religion in your life?

What is the source of your financial income?

What is your favorite hobby or leisure interest?

What do you feel most ashamed of in your past?

What is your grade-point average at present?

Have you ever cheated on exams?

Have you deliberately lied about a serious matter to either parent?

What is the most serious lie you have told?

How do you feel about couples living together without being married?

Have you ever experienced premarital or extramarital sex?

Do you practice masturbation?

Have you been arrested or fined for violating any law?

Have you any health problems? What are they?

Have you ever had a mystical experience?

What do you regard as your chief personality fault?

What turns you on the most?

How do you feel about interracial dating or marriage?

Do you consider yourself a political liberal or conservative?

What turns you off the fastest?

What features of your appearance do you consider most attractive to members of the opposite sex?

What do you regard as your least attractive features?

How important is money to you?

Are you or your parents divorced? Have you ever considered divorce?

What person would you most like to take a trip with right now?

How do you feel about swearing?

Have you ever been drunk?

Do you smoke marijuana or use drugs?

Do you enjoy manipulating or directing people?

Are females equal, inferior, or superior to males?

How often have you needed to see a doctor in the past year?

Have you ever been tempted to kill yourself?

Have you ever been tempted to kill someone else?

Would you participate in a public demonstration?

What emotions do you find most difficult to control?

Is there a particular person you wish would be attracted to you? Who?

What foods do you most dislike?

What are you most reluctant to discuss now?

To what person are you responding the most and how?

What's your IQ?

Is there any feature of your personality that you are proud of? What is it?

What was your worst failure, your biggest disappointment to yourself or family?

What is your favorite TV program(s)?

What is the subject of the most serious quarrels you have had with your parents?

What is the subject of your most frequent daydreams?

How are you feeling about me?

What are your career goals?

With what do you feel the greatest need for help?

What were you most punished or criticized for when you were a child?

How do you feel about crying in the presence of others?

Do you have any misgivings about the group so far?

What is your main complaint about the group?

Have you ever engaged in homosexual activities?

Do you like your name?

If you could be anything or anyone—besides yourself—what or who would you be?

Whom in your group don't you like?

Structured Experience 70

71. LEMONS: A SENSORY-AWARENESS ACTIVITY

Goal

> To increase sensory awareness.

Group Size

> Eight to twelve participants.

Time Required

> One hour.

Materials

> A lemon for each participant.

Physical Setting

> A large enough space for participants to sit comfortably in a circle on the floor.

Process

I. The facilitator asks the participants to sit on the floor in a large circle. He gives a lemon to each participant and explains that since no two lemons are identical, each person is to get to know his special lemon very well.

II. The facilitator allows the participants ten minutes to "become acquainted" with their lemons. They should spend the first five minutes observing the visual qualities of their lemons and the second five minutes, with their eyes closed, sensing through touch the unique tactile qualities of their lemons.

III. After ten minutes, the facilitator asks the participants to form dyads. Each member of a dyad then "introduces" his lemon to his partner by acquainting him with its particular characteristics.

IV. The facilitator then asks the dyad partners to exchange lemons and feel them to note the differences.

V. The facilitator now groups the dyads into intermediate groups of four or six. He asks the members of each new group to form a small circle and to place their lemons in a pile in the middle. He then asks them to close their eyes and to find their own lemons.

VI. The facilitator asks all participants again to form a large circle. He then collects the lemons and redistributes them to the participants. He asks the participants to close their eyes and pass the lemons to their right, feeling each one in order to identify their own. When a participant has identified his lemon, he is to put it in his lap and continue passing lemons until all participants have their own lemons.

VII. The facilitator discusses the experience with the group members, eliciting their reactions to utilizing the sensory skills involved.

Variations

I. Other fruits besides lemons can be used.

II. The entire process can be carried out nonverbally.

III. Step V can be eliminated.

IV. In step VI the lemons can be piled in the center of the room, and participants can be instructed to find theirs with their eyes open.

Similar Structured Experiences: *Vol. I:* Structured Experience **19, 22;** *Vol. II:* **24;** *Vol. III:* **72.**

Notes on the use of "Lemons":

72. NONVERBAL COMMUNICATION: A COLLECTION

Although numerous techniques in human relations training supplement and enhance learning that results from verbal interaction, nonverbal techniques (NVT's) also have become popular with both facilitators and laboratory participants. As Mill and Ritvo° point out, however, the potentialities of NVT's may be counterbalanced by a number of pitfalls. They suggest as guidelines three questions which the facilitator should be able to answer with "some sophistication":

1. How does your selection and use of an NVT fit into your understanding of the way people change (learning theory)?

2. What position does this NVT hold in the context of the laboratory goals toward which you are working (training design)?

3. What immediate and observable needs does this NVT meet, at this time and with these participants (specific relevance)?

As with each structured experience in these volumes, the verbal exploration which follows the NVT is at least as important as the experience itself if the application of laboratory learning is to be insured. When using NVT's, therefore, it seems doubly important to allow ample time to process data generated.

1. *Sticks and Stones.* Dowel rods and golfball-sized stones are placed in the center of the group, and members are told to use them, without talking, in any way appropriate to convey their reactions to each other.

2. *Posture Feedback.* One group member at a time receives nonverbal feedback: All other members assume body postures that indicate their impressions of him. There is a processing session after each member has received his feedback.

3. *Sociogram.* Group members form a living sociogram by placing and moving themselves and each other around the room in ways that are meaningful to them. The final form of the sociogram is drawn on newsprint and then discussed.

4. *Drum Dance.* Someone plays drums (or a recording of drums) while group members dance freely. Suddenly the drums are stopped, participants freeze for a moment, observe each other, and then pair off to discuss their observations.

°C. Mill and M. Ritvo, "Potentialities and Pitfalls of Nonverbal Techniques," *Human Relations Training News* 13, No. 1 (1969), 1-3.

5. *Body Talk.* Group members take turns trying to express various emotions with their bodies. The facilitator hands a participant a slip of paper indicating both the name of a feeling and the part of the body which he should use to express that emotion. Other participants try to guess the feeling expressed. (Examples: fright, anger, sexual attraction, boredom.)

6. *Red Rovers.* Participants form two lines facing each other. The persons at the head of each line cross over to the end (tail) of the opposite line. After all members have had this experience, collisions and styles of aggression and avoidance are discussed.

Similar Structured Experiences: *Vol. I:* Structured Experience **20, 22;** *Vol. II:* **44;** *Vol. III:* **71;** *'72 Annual:* **86;** *'73 Annual:* **90;** *Vol. IV:* **106.**
Lecturette Source: *'72 Annual:* "Modes of Communication: An Experiential Lecture."

Notes on the use of "Nonverbal Communication":

Structured Experience 72

73. WAHOO CITY: A ROLE ALTERNATION

Goals

I. To experience the dynamics of an alternate, unaccustomed role in a situation of community (or organization) conflict.

II. To develop skills in conflict resolution, negotiation, and problem-solving.

III. To introduce process analysis and feedback as necessary community (or organization) development techniques.

Group Size

A minimum of sixteen participants.

Time Required

A minimum of two hours.

Materials

I. Wahoo City Summary of Events Sheet for each of the four clusters.

II. A different Wahoo City Role-Description Sheet and its accompanying Additional Information Summary Sheet for each cluster.

III. Wahoo City Special Information Input for cluster 1.

IV. To designate clusters: signs and name tags in four different colors.

Physical Setting

A room large enough to accommodate clusters comfortably for small group discussion. A central arrangement of chairs and a table for the representatives' meetings. (Clusters may meet in separate rooms for their planning and discussion sessions.)

Process

I. The facilitator discusses goals, focusing on learning by assuming another role.

II. Four clusters are formed by participants volunteering to play roles they would not ordinarily assume. They go to the part of the room designated as their "turf" by a sign (e.g., City Manager's Office). Name tags designating members of each cluster are distributed.

III. A Summary of Events Sheet and a Role Description Sheet are given to each cluster, and time is allowed to read the information.

IV. The facilitator may spend some time helping the cluster members assume their roles by answering questions and suggesting alternative behaviors.

V. The facilitator may wish to address the entire group, emphasizing the following points:

    1. The need for participants to "play it straight" by carrying out their role responsibilities as authentically as possible.

    2. The accountability of representatives to the cluster.

    3. The need to be creative in order to maximize learning.

VI. The facilitator then distributes the appropriate Additional Information Summary Sheet to each cluster. He announces that a representatives' meeting will be held in fifteen minutes.

VII. The facilitator moves the group through the following stages:

    1. First cluster planning session in step VI preceding (fifteen minutes).

    2. First representatives' meeting (fifteen minutes).

    3. Giving of Special Information Input to cluster 1.

    4. Second cluster session, first half for processing the representatives' meeting (fifteen minutes).

    5. Second cluster session, second half for planning and strategy (fifteen minutes).

    6. Second representatives' meeting (fifteen minutes).

VIII. The facilitator stops the exercise. Each cluster is given fifteen minutes to process its functioning. All participants should then be seated in a large circle to share their learning and to process the whole exercise.

Variations

I. The same structure can be used with a different content.

II. Any number of special inputs—rumors, telephone messages, telegrams, etc.—can be introduced into the cluster meetings.

III. Clusters may be reconstituted after step VII number 4, with participants volunteering to play new roles.

Similar Structured Experiences: *Vol. I:* Structured Experience **9, 12;** *Vol. II:* **34, 41;** *Vol. III:* **68;** *'72 Annual:* **83;** *'73 Annual:* **98.**
Lecturette Sources: *'73 Annual:* "Win-Lose Situations," "Conditions Which Hinder Effective Communication," "Confrontation: Types, Conditions, and Outcomes," "Planned Renegotiation—A Norm-Setting OD Intervention."

Notes on the use of "Wahoo City":

Submitted by Peter Lawson, training consultant, Indianapolis, Indiana.

WAHOO CITY SUMMARY OF EVENTS SHEET

The following summarizes events which led to the present crisis, as reported in the *Wahoo City Press-Citizen* and the *Daily Wahoo.*

9/15—Four UW students were badly beaten by two carloads of gang members. One student was critically wounded and may suffer permanent partial paralysis. Gang members were reported as saying they were going to "clean up the University."

9/17—At 10:00 p.m. last night, two carloads of men attacked UW students on the campus. A coed, the daughter of a Plain City university official, reports phone calls threatening to "kill all the freaks."

9/20—A bomb threat was phoned today to the Director of Athletics at UW. The football game with State is in danger from bombers. The Director was quoted as saying, "We'll play the game in an empty stadium if necessary."

9/20—Arson attempts were made last night at the UW Art Museum and the UW Library. "SDS" was painted on buildings. Police have "suspects" but refuse to divulge whether or not they are university students.

9/22—Eleven UW students were attacked last night in three separate incidents. "Hard hats" were allegedly present. The attackers said, "We're cleaning up the campus," according to one victim. Another victim, a UW graduate student, accused police of "total neglect and disinterest" in pursuing alleged attackers.

The *Daily Wahoo* reported an increasing number of cars cruising the UW campus. An editorial called for concerted police action.

A television news interview indicated that the City Police, according to the Chief, "have no leads at all on the attacks on students."

9/23—Three UW students were admitted to the hospital following daylight beatings by men "cleaning up things." The UW Faculty Senate today condemned the vigilante attacks and called for swift police action.

9/24—A "Peace Party Picnic and Rock Festival" on the UW Men's Athletic Field was marked by violence as "hard hats" waded into the crowd. Twenty-two students were treated for injuries. A UW faculty member who witnessed the beatings accused the City Police and Campus Security personnel of "turning their backs." The Vice-President of the UW Young Republicans alleged that police undercover agents recorded the event on both still and movie cameras.

A *Wahoo City Press-Citizen* by-lined report indicated that no arrests in the incident were made by any police personnel. Three students were booked following the picnic for unlawful possession of marijuana.

Structured Experience 73

WAHOO CITY ROLE-DESCRIPTION SHEET: CLUSTER 1

DATE: 9/25

You are the *City Manager's Office.* You are here to discuss plans for a meeting that you have called for this afternoon. You have invited representatives from the UW Provost's Office, the Wahoo City Student Coalition, and the Citizens for Concerted Action to lay plans for meeting the crisis that has been developing over the last several weeks. The noon editions of the *Wahoo City Press-Citizen* and the *Daily Wahoo* have reported plans for a protest rally to be held on the steps of Bower Hall this evening. The potential for violence is great.

ADDITIONAL INFORMATION SUMMARY SHEET: CLUSTER 1

In addition to press reports, you have the following information:

1. The County Sheriff has said that his men will not deal with the situation. "The duty rests with the City and County Police and with Campus Security."

2. The City Police Chief has said privately that he believes the situation could best be handled by the University administration. "All they have to do is use the new Code to get rid of all the radical students and faculty." He will not act on the campus without the official written request of the University administration.

3. Informants report that "hard hats" may be behind the bomb threats and arson attempts and that the SDS is planning to shut down the University with a student strike.

4. The City Manager has been notified that the Lincoln State Police (Plain City) have put all personnel on riot alert. State Police Headquarters has also indicated in an official message that forty men have been moved into the Ramada Inn in Wahoo.

5. The Governor's Administrative Assistant has made several phone calls, checking on the situation to keep the Governor informed in case the National Guard has to be called up.

WAHOO CITY ROLE-DESCRIPTION SHEET: CLUSTER 2

DATE: 9/25

You are the *UW Provost's Office*. You are meeting to prepare your plans and strategies for a meeting which has been called for this afternoon by the City Manager to discuss the crisis which has been developing over the last several weeks. The noon editions of the *Wahoo City Press-Citizen* and the *Daily Wahoo* have reported plans for a protest rally on the steps of Bower Hall this evening. The potential for violence is great.

ADDITIONAL INFORMATION SUMMARY SHEET: CLUSTER 2

In addition to press reports, you have the following information:

1. An increasing number of parents have been pressing for better protection for their children. Thirty-two women students have been withdrawn from the University by their parents.

2. The Legislature has been applying pressure to assure that the University will remain open.

3. The Regents have underscored the necessity of upholding the new Code of Student and Faculty Conduct.

4. Campus Security has reported an increasing incidence of "hard hats" cruising the campus in cars.

5. Academic department chairmen report that class attendance has dropped off markedly, particularly among women students.

Structured Experience 73

WAHOO CITY ROLE-DESCRIPTION SHEET: CLUSTER 3

DATE: 9/25

You are the *Citizens for Concerted Action*, an informal group formed under the auspices of the Church Federation, the United Fund Agency, and the Association of Neighborhood Councils to deal with the polarization and hostility developing in the city.

You are meeting to discuss the crisis which has been developing the last several weeks. The City Manager has asked you to send a representative to a meeting in his office this afternoon. The noon editions of the *Wahoo City Press-Citizen* and the *Daily Wahoo* have reported plans for a protest rally on the steps of Bower Hall this evening. The potential for violence is great.

ADDITIONAL INFORMATION SUMMARY SHEET: CLUSTER 3

In addition to press reports, you have the following information:

1. Rumor: The President of the University is in ill health.
2. Rumor: The football game may be switched to Plain City because of the bomb threat.

WAHOO CITY ROLE-DESCRIPTION SHEET: CLUSTER 4

-- ....

DATE: 9/25

You are the *Wahoo City Student Coalition*, an association of student organizations on the UW campus. You are meeting to make preparations for sending a representative to a meeting in the City Manager's office this afternoon to discuss the crisis that has been developing over the last several weeks. The noon editions of the *Wahoo City Press-Citizen* and the *Daily Wahoo* have reported plans for a protest rally to be held on the steps of Bower Hall this evening. The potential for violence is great.

-- ....

ADDITIONAL INFORMATION SUMMARY SHEET: CLUSTER 4

In addition to press reports, you have the following information:

1. The arsonists are not students or SDS members, but "hard hats."
2. The SDS, which is not represented in the Coalition, has been calling for a student strike for better police protection. The SDS is saying that the University should shut down unless and until students can be properly protected.
3. Rumor: There are a lot of guns in the dorms.
4. The Provost's Office, in line with Regents' policy, has made it very clear that individuals who violate the new Code will be subject to immediate cancellation of registration.

-- ....

Structured Experience 73

WAHOO CITY SPECIAL INFORMATION INPUT

THE GOVERNOR'S OFFICE
Plain City, Lincoln

September 25, 1973

The City Manager
Wahoo City, Lincoln

Dear Sir:

Reports in the press indicate a growing crisis in Wahoo City.

My staff has given me hourly reports on the situation, and
I am increasingly concerned over the seeming lack of control on
the part of the University and the City Administration.

A report that has just come to my desk from the State Police
Intelligence Unit indicates that there will be a serious and
violent confrontation this evening. I am convinced of the accuracy
of this report.

I am therefore, as Chief of State, issuing orders that the
National Guard be called up and dispatched to Wahoo City to assume
martial law.

Brigadier General Scott Williams will be in command of the
operation. You will no doubt hear from him presently. He has
assured me that Guard units will be in Wahoo City and on
patrol within the next four hours.

I have sent word of my action to the Regents and to the
President of Wahoo University. I have also notified the
Chief of Police of Wahoo City and the County Sheriff by
copy of this order.

Sincerely,

Ronald E. Neumann
Governor of Lincoln

74. PERSONAL JOURNAL: A SELF-EVALUATION

Goals

I. To heighten participants' awareness of the sequence of events and the corresponding emotional development which takes place in a laboratory or a workshop.

II. To aid in self-disclosure.

III. To provide a post-laboratory or post-workshop resource for reinforcing learning.

Group Size

Unlimited.

Time Required

Any number of periods of ten to fifteen minutes each, depending on the design of the laboratory or workshop.

Materials

I. Pencils.

II. A spiral-bound notebook for each participant.

Physical Setting

Participants should be provided with tables or other writing surfaces which enable them to sit a short distance from each other while making entries in their notebooks.

Process

I. The facilitator introduces the concept of personal-journal-keeping as a way of understanding better the learning and experiences that will take place during the laboratory or workshop.

II. He gives each participant a notebook and a pencil.

III. He asks the participants to use the left-hand pages of the notebook for objective descriptions of the process of the group and the right-hand pages for subjective reactions to the process described. He may wish to post a typical journal entry, such as the following:

What Happened	How I Felt
John began by using a getting-acquainted exercise in which we were to list ten facts about ourselves under the title "Who am I?" We were to pin on the list and then walk around reading other people's lists without talking.	I felt a little panicked at first because nothing came to mind but "vice-president in charge of sales." Then I thought of several silly things I might write, but I wasn't sure I wanted all these people to see them.

IV. The facilitator explains that participants will be given time during the laboratory or workshop to make entries in the journal.

Variations

I. The facilitator may wish to use the journals along with the "Johari Window" or the "Dyadic Encounter" (*Vol. I*: Structured Experiences 13 and 21) as a means of encouraging self-disclosure. He may wish to form "Helping Pairs" (*Vol. II*: Structured Experience 45), who meet to process the subjective material.

II. As part of closing activities, the facilitator may wish to have participants graph their subjective responses during the entire laboratory or workshop, to refocus on peak experiences and to get a sense of what the group experience has meant for them.

III. Periodically the journal entries can be duplicated with carbon paper so that the staff can use the carbon copies as a barometer of the training effects.

Similar Structured Experiences: *Vol. II:* Structured Experience **40, 46**; *'73 Annual:* **100.**
Lecturette Sources: *'73 Annual:* "Thinking and Feeling," "Value Clarification."

Notes on the use of "Personal Journal":

SOURCES OF ADDITIONAL STRUCTURED EXPERIENCES

Gunther, B. *Sense Relaxation: Below Your Mind.* New York: Collier Books, 1968.

Gunther, B. *What to Do Till the Messiah Comes.* New York: Collier Books, 1971.

James, M., and D. Jongeward. *Born to Win: Transactional Analysis with Gestalt Experiments.* Reading, Mass.: Addison-Wesley, 1971.

Jones, J.E., and J.W. Pfeiffer. *The 1973 Annual Handbook for Group Facilitators.* University Associates, 1973.

Lewis, H., and H. Streitfield. *Growth Games.* New York: Bantam, 1971.

Maier, N.R.F., A.R. Solem, and A.A. Maier. *Supervisory and Executive Development: A Manual for Role Playing.* New York: Wiley, 1967.

Malamud, D.I., and S. Machover. *Toward Self-Understanding: Group Techniques in Self-Confrontation.* Springfield, Ill.: Thomas, 1965.

NTL Institute for Applied Behavioral Science. *Twenty Exercises for Trainers.* Washington, D.C., 1972.

Nylen, D., J.R. Mitchell, and A. Stout (editors). *Handbook of Staff Development and Human Relations Training: Materials Developed for Use in Africa* (revised edition). Washington, D.C.: NTL Institute for Applied Behavioral Science, 1967.

Otto, H.A. *Group Methods to Actualize Human Potential: A Handbook* (second edition). Beverly Hills: Holistic Press, 1970.

Pfeiffer, J.W., and R. Heslin. *Instrumentation in Human Relations Training: A Guide to 75 Instruments with Wide Application to the Behavioral Sciences.* University Associates, 1973.

Pfeiffer, J.W., and J.E. Jones. *A Handbook of Structured Experiences for Human Relations Training, Volumes I* (revised), *II* (revised), *and IV.* University Associates, 1974, 1974, and 1973.

Pfeiffer, J.W., and J.E. Jones. *The 1972 Annual Handbook for Group Facilitators.* University Associates, 1972.

Satir, V. *Conjoint Family Therapy: A Guide to Theory and Technique.* Palo Alto, Ca.: Science and Behavior Books, 1967.

Schmuck, R.A., P.J. Runkel, *et al. Handbook of Organization Development in Schools.* Palo Alto, Ca.: National Press Books, 1972.

Schutz, W.C. *Joy: Expanding Human Awareness.* New York: Grove Press, 1967.

Please add the following name to your mailing list.

_____

_____

_____

_____ Zip _____

Primary Organizational Affiliation: ☐ fill in with one
number from below

1. Education
2. Business & Industry
3. Religious Organization
4. Government Agency
5. Counseling

6. Mental Health
7. Community, Voluntary, and/or
   Service Organization
8. Health Care
9. Library
0. Consulting

Please add the following name to your mailing list.

_____

_____

_____

_____ Zip _____

Primary Organizational Affiliation: ☐ fill in with one
number from below

1. Education
2. Business & Industry
3. Religious Organization
4. Government Agency
5. Counseling

6. Mental Health
7. Community, Voluntary, and/or
   Service Organization
8. Health Care
9. Library
0. Consulting

|||||

NO POSTAGE
NECESSARY
IF MAILED
IN THE
UNITED STATES

BUSINESS REPLY CARD
FIRST CLASS   PERMIT NO. 11201 SAN DIEGO, CA

POSTAGE WILL BE PAID BY ADDRESSEE

University Associates, Inc.
8517 Production Avenue
P.O. Box 26240
San Diego, California 92126

|||||

NO POSTAGE
NECESSARY
IF MAILED
IN THE
UNITED STATES

BUSINESS REPLY CARD
FIRST CLASS   PERMIT NO. 11201 SAN DIEGO, CA

POSTAGE WILL BE PAID BY ADDRESSEE

University Associates, Inc.
8517 Production Avenue
P.O. Box 26240
San Diego, California 92126